Religion in a Technical Age

SAMUEL H. MILLER

Religion in

HARVARD UNIVERSITY PRESS

a Technical Age

CAMBRIDGE, MASSACHUSETTS   1968

TO MY COLLEAGUES OF THE HARVARD DIVINITY
SCHOOL, WITH GRATITUDE AND AFFECTION

Preface

Theological education cannot be isolated from the general religious troubles of our age. Everything that has disturbed the faith of men in our time is accentuated at the point where we try to train men and women to guide others in a vitally reverent way of life. All the changing currents of tumultous history run through the human heart, where they must be evaluated and the meaning of life itself discerned. Such whirlpools and riptides make self-assurance difficult to attain. With the impact of three centuries of scientific theory and practice, the shattering effects of two world wars, the general loss of order, belief, and intrinsic authority, religion has found itself torn between an easy conformity to the past which ignores the present and an agonizing attempt to elicit meaning from the present without repudiating the past.

Under such conditions, there is an unusual temptation to use education as a world of its own, in which "the uncontaminated intellect may delight in its own erudition." The end result is what Rousseau referred to as the "immorality of knowledge."

Religion, and in our case, theological education, cannot rest content with an abstract sophistication, for we are concerned with people, people at their most complex, subtle and mysterious level of existence, where they brush against the transcendent realities which are so elusive, so hard to locate, and so difficult to talk about. What are the means, in theology or history or biology, to put men's feet on a path of faith which, if they keep on walking, will bring them in reach of the eternal verities? In all the confusion of this mad mad world, where the landmarks are gone or twisted, where the noise and incessant change have become frightening, our job is to educate men to identify for themselves the realities of faith in their own experience, and by teaching or preaching or pastoring, to assist others to do the same. Because the human condition generally is unsettled, and because our primary point of reference is the human being, whether he is the student preparing for religious leadership or the parishioner who will be subject to it, our program of education must take into account such nonacademic forces.

The stubborn faith which men once had in religion has increasingly shifted in America to education. For a long time we assumed it would solve all our problems, if not immediately, then surely in a little time. To behold the massive invasion of schools at every level, and the enormous expansion at college and graduate levels, is to see a fantastic spectacle. Obviously our faith in education has not dwindled.

And yet it is equally plain that there is a violent refusal to accept education in its present state as satisfactory. On all sides changes are in order, radical experiments are being tried, and traditions are being wrenched loose by the powerful forces of cultural revolution. There are student riots and faculty surveys, federal subsidies and community conflicts, all rising from an effort to reshape the body of this major instrument of society.

In the professional schools the climate has been more conservative. In business and engineering, new professions of more recent origin, there were fewer stereotypes inherited from the past. In medicine, law, and the ministry, the traditions were longer and more deeply entrenched. But both medicine and law have made their accommodation to the revolutions of contemporary culture in a way religion has not. Put on the defensive by a series of mistaken nineteenth-century gestures, the ministry has detoured around the essential revision of its role and sought to maintain itself by an ingratiating but unprofessional popularity.

It is in the light of such a long-delayed transformation of the ministry and its theological training that the addresses and essays in this book were written. Given at different occasions across the country during the last seven years, they may seem to shift abruptly from one chapter to the next. Yet I hope there is sufficient in common to justify their inclusion under the total vision of our present situation and the task which it entails.

S.H.M.

Contents

Religion in a Technical Age

RELIGION IN A TECHNICAL AGE

Atechnical age is a new thing. There have been ages, to be sure, characterized by the invention of the wheel, or of gunpowder, or of the steam engine, but these all left the bulk of man's life untouched. The broad stream of man's ways flowed on unimpeded, much as it had been before they were discovered. They were innovations which interrupted his world only here and there, leaving the main body of it preponderantly the same. In the last century, however, we have seen the elaboration of technical facilities and their use literally explode with such astonishing extensiveness that no portion of human experience, however intimate, has not been invaded. For the first time in human history, the totality of man's environment has been permeated by technical devices and, to a large extent, controlled by them.

Modern man has come to accept the "method of technique" as the quickest and surest answer to every problem. There are techniques of research, techniques of prayer, techniques of sex, techniques of counseling and of communication, techniques of skiing, hair-styling, embalming, gardening, cattle raising, and gaining friends—everything thinkable has been reduced to a technique, a "how to do it" pattern guaranteed to work. It is in truth a technical age, thoroughly habituated to expect that there is a technique to meet every need.

This is not only a new thing in itself, but it has created a new form of society—massive agglomerations of people in vast city complexes, which we have begun to call "megalopolises." Unlike the cities of other ages, these are held together by enormous networks of technicized communication and trans-

Given as the Presidential Lecture at the University of Connecticut, Storrs, Connecticut, March 29, 1966.

portation systems. Something of the precariousness of these supporting fabrics has been brought home to us in the recent blackout and the subway strike.

Not only is the megalopolis sustained by these technical means, but what appears as rural country, the village and the farm, has become part and parcel of the urban culture. Automobiles have opened up one-time secluded or isolated areas; shopping centers are as common as churches, TV and radio are as much a part of instant culture in the farthest back hinterland as in the most congested city. Geographically, everything has been drawn into the city-society.

Moreover, the coverage of this technical facility in communications and transportation has been universalized. It has not only created the outsize city, the city-society, but it has penetrated the entire world and made it over into an inescapably intimate neighborhood. A whole world of happenings, from dog fights to the fall of empires, is seen and heard at the same time. Whatever happens anywhere affects people everywhere. Although not morally or emotionally united, it is a technically united world. The strain between the measure of our hearts and the measure of our technical know-how represents our severe uneasiness and not altogether hidden fear that our very success at one level may be our undoing at another.

The second novelty in this new age is a kind of politics. It is no longer sufficient to "represent" the people. Government is no longer merely political in the traditional sense of the word, but has moved into economics, industry, medicine, education, agriculture, and welfare in a rapid proliferation. The technical facilities at hand provide both an opportunity and a demand to "plan" for the people, to control the economy, and to distribute and redistribute national resources for their health, education, and security in such a way as to support the largest margins of prosperity and comfort. This requires a huge establishment of experts and an enormous massing of financial resources. The new politics is as different from its traditional antecedents as the atom bomb is from the crossbow.

The third consequence of technicity is a new method of work. Once a man learned a skill, became an artisan or craftsman by the disciplines of his own body and vision, developed through a lifetime of persevering self-criticism, and then passed it on to his sons. Meantime, he possessed a concrete role in the community of human needs. Today the technical power and facility of machines has taken precedence over the old order of individual craftsmen. Production has been escalated by utilizing uniformity of design and by effective use of the assembly line. Man, once *homo faber,* has now become *homo technicus,* a species of interchangeable parts subject to the needs of the mechanical process of manufacture. Moreover, such methods have led to overproduction in almost every area of industry, so that continued operation depends on built-in obsolescence and forced propaganda to maximize the market. Even with these unquestionably ethical methods, cyclical unemployment forces the political government to assume an economic role of taking up the slack whenever it occurs.

In the fourth place, we have a new kind of culture; we generally call it "mass culture." Once entertainment was local and communal, in the form of holidays or fairs, supporting the common experience in the home or in the village. Now our pleasure tends to be *en masse;* it takes place over the entire nation, or the continent, or even the entire globe. While it is everywhere at the same time, it is no longer domestic or communal. Indeed, one of its deficiencies is that it is nonparticipatory. It is spectatorial, and because it is linked with commercial propaganda concerned with exciting the largest possible number of the more gullible part of the population, it is degraded to appeal to the most venial propensities of humanity.

In the fifth place, a new intensity has sprung into being between the individual and society. This is profoundly complex and ambiguous. The catchwords signalizing the crisis are "alienation," "loneliness," "beatnik," "age of anxiety," "organization man," and so on. The massive weight of an extended society has not been easy to bear. Our literature and drama, as well as our mental institutions, give ample evidence of the excessive strain put upon a basic and perennial tug of war to which Sigmund Freud called attention over and over again. The more massive society has become, the less able it has been to support us with vital relationships or with a substantive meaning of life. When we have willingly conformed to its frenzied and compulsive dynamics, we have been disillusioned and exhausted. Conspicuous consumption, unparalleled supply of temporary status symbols, elusive labels of success with little stability or contentment, have led to very little satisfaction. The symbols derived from a technical order have no depth or richness sufficient to match and vitalize the mysteries of life at the human level. Ultimately, wherever we have committed ourselves to a spontaneous and enthusiastic slavery to technical ends, a profound and vigorous hostility overtakes us, exacerbates our aggressive instincts, and spreads to all levels and areas of our life, expressing itself indirectly, neurotically, destructively, in marriage, between the generations, and often in ways disguised from ourselves.

These are what might be called the gross effects of the technological revolution. Many living in it have not yet discerned the human significance of what has already been accomplished. Four professors of the Harvard Business School, writing in a study of industrialism and the industrial man, have said, "In our times it is no longer the spectre of Communism which is haunting Europe, but rather emerging industrialization in many forms that is confronting the whole world. The giant of industrialism is stalking the earth, transforming almost all the features of older and traditional societies." [1] We have vast collectivities, but no community; we have politics largely concerned with stabilizing and planning for the economic security and comfort of the population; we have a new method of work in which the creative quality of a man is lost, or at least obscured; we have a new kind of pleasure, which is scarcely culture, in the sense of sustaining the mind and heart with a vision of reality, but rather is used to fill up or waste free time; and, finally, we have a new intensity of individual and collective violence, which we enjoy vicariously, or in actual conflict.

It is little wonder, despite America's general enthusiasm for anything new or anything technical, that we have had a divided mind about the roaring progress of the technical revolution. At least our writers and philosophers have not been very easy about it. Thomas Jefferson declared, "I dread the day when all the people are piled one upon the other in the cities." Henry Thoreau's crabbed cynicism about the railroad that ran through his Eden at Walden Pond is too well known to repeat. Nor does one need to look twice at Mark Twain's epic comedy of Huck Finn to see the fear and ferocity the author displayed in the face of encroaching technocracy. Nearer our time, William Faulkner was to display the same dismay in the story "The Bear," where man's civilization slowly invades and destroys not only the primeval land but all its virtues. Similarly, Ernest Hemingway inveighs bitterly at the onslaught of technical machines as they rip and tear the earth. These, of course, are all "romantics," quite elemental romantics, in the sense of standing between the primeval land, the Eden of innocence, and the ruthless machinery of urban civili-

[1] Clark Kerr, J. T. Dunlop, F. H. Harbison, and C. A. Myers, *Industrialism and Industrial Man: The Problem of Labor and Management in Economic Growth* (Cambridge, Massachusetts: Harvard University Press, 1960).

zation. But there have been more frightening visions of what it might mean if the technical age moves into its full political implementation as in George Orwell's 1984, or Huxley's *Brave New World*, or David Karp's *One*. Harold Rosenberg has declared that "the fall was not in Eden, but in the 19th century when machinery was introduced." There the struggle reaches nightmare proportions as man himself in his essential humanity is threatened with extinction.

Indeed, let us not be too sanguine. The very measure of our technical controls has reached a new category of power. The technical means are available to realize Huxley's fiction in the synthetic production of Alpha pluses or intellectuals, and epsilon minus or laborers, by variations of the nutrient medium in a Petri dish. We are transplanting organs from body to body. We are ready to stimulate the brain to receive ten times its present capacity and to retain it ten times longer. We are inducing religious states of revelation with the aid of hallucinogenic drugs. There are subtler influences which are not so obvious and yet in the long run may be more deleterious from the point of view of religion and the spirit of man. As Carlyle pungently expressed it, "Not the external and physical alone is managed now by machinery; but the internal and spiritual also . . . The same habit regulates not our modes of action alone, but our modes of thought and feeling. Men are grown mechanical in head and in heart, as well as in hand." An indication of this from an ancient text from the Far East may illustrate this matter at a primitive but nonetheless perceptive level:

When Tsi Gung came into the region north of the river Han, he saw an old man busy in his vegetable garden. He had dug ditches for watering. He himself climbed into the well, brought up a container full of water in his arms, and emptied it. He exerted himself to the utmost, but achieved very little.

Tsi Gung spoke: "There is an arrangement with which it is

possible to fill a hundred ditches with water every day. With little effort much is accomplished. Wouldn't you like to use it?" The gardener rose up, looked at him and said, "What would that be?"

Tsi Gung said, "A lever is used, weighted at one end and light at the other. In this way water can be drawn, so that it gushes out. It is known as a draw-well."

At that, anger rose up in the face of the old man, and he laughed, saying, "I have heard my teacher say: 'When a man uses a machine he carries on all his business in a machine-like manner. Whoever does his business in the manner of a machine develops a machine heart. Whoever has a machine heart in his breast loses his simplicity. Whoever loses his simplicity becomes uncertain in the impulses of his spirit. Uncertainty in the impulses of the spirit is something that is incompatible with truth.' Not that I am unfamiliar with such devices; I am ashamed to use them." [2]

The phrase, "Whoever loses his simplicity becomes uncertain in the impulses of his spirit," has particular cogency for our condition. This spiritual uncertainty in our time has become endemic to the whole society. We are at a loss to say where we are religiously. We do not know what we believe. The outlines of traditional conviction have been softened, and we prefer to float about in this blurred climate. Respectability, the outer façade of repute, has hardened, but religion itself has grown vague, so vague indeed that there seems no vocabulary left in which to talk intelligibly about God.

One of the most startling effects of the technical age upon religion is the subtle influences of speed. As Gabriel Marcel has remarked, there is something inimical to the spirit in speed. Speed develops its own mystique, its own satisfactions. It is

[2] Werner Heisenberg, "The Representation of Nature in Contemporary Physics." Originally published in *Die Künste im Technischen Zeitalter* on behalf of the Bavarian Academy of Fine Arts (Munich: R. Oldenbourg, 1956). Reprinted in *Daedalus,* Summer 1958.

generated by the machine and by a peculiar nemesis, human beings assume the accelerated tempo of the technical apparatus until it becomes compulsive. The final result, when speed is extrapolated in all of man's activities, beginning with his business and industry, where it can be justified, and extending into his play, his leisure, his education, where it can scarcely be judged appropriate, is a thoroughly unreflective manner of haste-ridden living. Religion does not thrive in such a climate; its roots need depth, and depth only comes from paying attention to things as they happen.

This blur, so to speak, comes not only from speed but also from one of the basic facts of the technical revolution. Wherever techniques become the ruling method for the solution of problems, both theoretical and practical, there we live in a world of means to the increasing exclusion of ends. This is precisely what seems to characterize our life. We are obsessed with the means, fascinated by the cleverness, the rapid application, the quick results, of the means, until we become so immersed in them we no longer ask ourselves what we are trying to attain. We love to ride in a car, even though we have no place to go; speed has its own mystique, regardless of destination or lack of destination.

So it is with organization. This is the speed technique of handling people. We organize everything, and we do it so well and with such thoroughness that we finally end up organizing for the sheer joy of it, without concerning ourselves with the "end" we have in view. Nowhere is this seen better than in the development of what we call a bureaucracy. This is organization which moves beyond the simple requirement of sustaining the order necessary for life or work, and elaborates itself, literally feeds upon itself, until it achieves a ponderous obesity of self-importance. The end has been obliterated in the multiplicity of means; indeed, at last the means become the end.

Having looked briefly at what the technical world has done to change the shape of man's world, we must ask what is the stance of religion in regard to it. What can or should religion try to do in this new kind of world? What is the proper function of faith and the church in such an environment? Do we remain as we were and hope the world some day will return to our way of thinking and doing things? Or do we throw over the past entirely and marry things as they are, for better or for worse, in a state of euphoric optimism?

There are temptations both ways. The present age is so exciting, so vital, so exuberant, and so dangerous that we are apt to rush in hastily to consecrate "secularity" as an unmixed blessing which leads to sheer conformity, however hidden it may be in the chaos of rapid change. Or, on the other hand, out of fright at such tumultous novelty, we revert to an obdurate hostility to the world and consecrate ourselves in our ecclesiastical self-sufficiency, as if God did not create the world or did not move through history, or as if the church could really separate itself from time and space in some kind of unholy presumption. The fact of the case is that both extremes are simplistic subterfuges. This age has tremendous deficiencies, which only religion can fill; religion is a failure if it has no power to redeem the age in which it exists. Our proper stance is complex, compounded of many dialectical tensions and mutual ambiguities. It is as Robert Frost said, a lover's quarrel with the world! Our humanity is woven inextricably into it, and there is no way for us to extract ourselves from it. The problem is to keep the reins in our hands and to see to it that things do not get in the saddle and ride us.

This lover's quarrel begins with what I believe can be called a critical openness. Faith is not foregone closure, nor is it sentimental credulity. The world is precisely a mixture; that is what makes it the world. The word became flesh; the Kingdom of God is among you; he became of no reputation—always and everywhere one must discern the acts of God amid the confusions of history. There are no convenient halos above the heads of saints as long as they do the will of God in this mortal world of easily mistaken appearances. Signs are not to be given to this or any generation—two men see the same event, but only one has the perceptiveness to know the meaning of what he sees.

So it is with this technical world. It is full to bursting with all kinds of contradictory possibilities. There is more freedom than ever, and more fear that it is precarious and easily lost. There is more prosperity, but dimly felt by multitudes is the hidden damnation, the smothering weight of too much of it. There is more power, but the humble joys of the skillful hand go unfulfilled. There is more free time, but less and less knowledge of how to use it, so there is really less true leisure. There is more variety, but less coherence; more information, but less wisdom; more speed, but less direction; more convenience, but less contentment; more ambition, but less satisfaction. And along with this mixed world, religion itself is mixed with its own contradictions of more respectability and less righteousness; more property and less passion; more numbers and fewer disciples; more organization and less sacrifice; more theology and less faith; more success and less sanctity; more security and less spirit.

Because it is a mixed-up world, the first task of religion in this technical age, as in any other, is to make discriminating judgments about the significance of things, to put a value on them with reasonable clarity and certainty. Every new age ushers in unprecedented forms and forces which need to be evaluated, put into some kind of order, and weighed in terms of their moral gravity. We have unprecedented power, as in the atom bomb, and it has not been worked into any morals system. We have unprecedented freedom, as in birth control, and it is waiting to be seriously socialized with a careful estimation of its consequences. We have unprecedented production, as in industry, and it has not yet been thought through in reference to an ethical disregard for the character of materials deliberately degraded by intent to obsolescence, or a similar disregard of the creative instincts of the worker. We have unprecedented free time, and will have more, but we have not known as yet how to save it from the degradation of compulsive frenzy by which time, as we say, is killed. One could extend the list, but fundamentally the business of religion is to penetrate these enlarged dimensions of the world and to give them a positive meaning. In the best sense of the term, this is the serious and creative work of the moral conscience.

If there is a positive dimension of "evangelizing" the new provinces opened up by the technical age, we should not shirk its negative aspects. Judgment must be made, made clearly and unequivocally, where the new forces operate with demonic destructiveness. I am not speaking now of slapping the moralistic stereotypes of a previous age upon our world; that does not represent either moral insight or religious sensibility. Rather the probity with which men of other ages sorted out the good and evil of their time needs to be translated into a new lucidity and soberness in assessing the novel forms of good and evil which have recently made their appearance in our time. Where things smother the spirit, where techniques obscure the ends, where the machine obliterates the human, and bureaucracy squeezes out every vestige of the soul's mystery, our voice must be clear, strong, and unmistakable. Where humanity is at stake, we cannot be less than bold.

Probably the most serious and perplexing level of this moral exercise of religion in the new provinces of our age is the requirement that we should be able to identify what I prefer to call "the unecclesiastical activity of God." One of the exciting aspects of this new age has been the renaissance of spiritual concern in many realms of our contemporary world. Not only has there appeared in the arts and literature the profound question of moral destiny, but in government and science and business and law a fresh and vigorous search for humanistic values and intimate meaning has broken out. The task of religion is to confirm the activity of God in the mixed arena of the world. Whatever it is that happens in church should provide us with the vision whereby we may see holiness in unexpected places and gladly celebrate it.

As a result of the exercise of such a moral imagination in weighing the character of our world, religion will inevitably confront a second step. We must produce a new kind of person. He must be able to shake himself free from the worn-out stereotypes and bold enough to step into the larger dimensions of freedom and power which the modern world has generated, and to do it with such lucid seriousness that both society and the individual will be aware of the rightness of what he does. He will be able to establish new norms of what it means to be human, to be open to the expanding life of creation, and at the same time discriminating enough to determine the direction of history. When Simone Weil says that we need a new saintliness in the world unlike any we have seen before, she is referring to this new kind of person. We must move into a new level of consciousness, a vaster and more sensitive conscience, an order of human greatness beyond the ordinary, if we are to meet the extended demands of a world reshaped by technical means.

The burden on human beings, on being human, is quite immeasurable. One can read it in the solemn seriousness of Robert Bolt's *A Man for All Seasons,* or in Arthur Miller's *Death of a Salesman,* or in Ionesco's *Rhinoceros,* or in Ghelderode's *Pantagleize.* One sees it in Camus' *The Fall,* or in

Silone's *Bread and Wine,* or in Musil's *Man Without Qualities.*
It shrieks in the sculptures of Cesar and Roszak and Paolozzi.
It writhes in anguish in Picasso's *Guernica.* It haunts the
imageless canvases of Mondrian and Kandinsky and Jackson
Pollack. The agony of the crucifixion in this century is manifested wherever man finds himself crushed by the inhuman
machinery of a technically obsessed world. Whether faith can
create the kind of man who can transcend such odds remains
to be seen. That we are under the hammer cannot be doubted.

Roderick Seidenberg, in *Post-Historic Man,* speaks of the
individual in the rising tide of industrialism as no longer necessary. Karl Jaspers speaks of the absorption of man in the
"apparatus." Gabriel Marcel describes the "techniques of degradation" by which man is reduced to functions. Whether
religion or the church can find some way to save man, to guard
his humanity, or conserve his essential self in the face of the
abrasions of a technical age, remains to be seen. But that it
is in a sense the most critical issue before the church, I do
not doubt. Yet for the most part the lumbering juggernaut of
ecclesiastical machinery is operating far from this crucial
agony of mankind. The traditional notion of salvation as the
saving of the soul as something apart from man's humanity
will need correction. What is in danger now is precisely man's
humanity. Unless we can save that, there is no sense in talking
about the soul.

There is a third point without which neither our critical openness can operate nor our will to create a new kind of person
can transform our present consciousness. It is the location of
a transcendent reality which will enable the moral imagination
to discriminate within a wise perspective, and by which a
man can become a new creature. Basically, there is no way
we can part company with our society except by some powerful
thrust of a believable transcendent; nor is there any way for

man to move beyond what he is to become what he needs to be except by the force of transcendence.

As Robert Bolt puts it, "It may be that a clear sense of the self can only crystallize round something transcendental, in which case our prospects look poor, for we are rightly committed to the rational. I think the paramount gift our thinkers, artists, and for all I know, our men of science, should labor to get for us is a sense of selfhood without resort to magic." [3]

If the self can only be maintained in its essential dignity by reference to some kind of transcendence, then religion must learn to speak with new lucidity and fresh excitement about God. We are going through an aggravating state of sloughing off respectable but uncritical stereotypes which we inherited from a much less sophisticated era. What amounted to an irreligious idolatry of hypocritical sentimentalism has fogged the vision of the true God for a century. Added to this has been the unfortunate intellectual indolence of American Protestantism, which failed to bring together the symbols of primordial revelation and the contemporary disclosures of science in the way men think of reality, both in the cosmic and the personal realms. We simply have not done our homework, and the problems in the day's quiz are making our ignorance embarrassingly plain. A technical age is as deficient in any attention paid to transcendence as it is to the question of ends; our task is to point out, with as much clarity and perceptiveness as we can muster, the reality of the transcendent in such a mixed world. Significantly enough, that is what has been going on for decades, both in the novel and on the stage. I wish I could say as much for the church! All that one can say is that the wineskins which held the exciting intoxication of the tran-

[3] Robert Bolt, in Preface to "A Man for All Seasons," in *The New Theatre of Europe,* Robert W. Corrigan, ed. (New York: Delta Original, Dell Publ. Co., 1962), p. 39.

scendent are still on view, empty and stiff, full of honor but of nothing else.

There is another aspect of the transcendent which is particularly elusive to define, but which always disappears when the transcendent fades from human consciousness, and when it goes, anxiety increases, violence erupts, order dissolves, and direction is lost. It is in the subtler substance of authority that transcendence makes itself known—not authority in a legal sense, or in the mere posture of power, or in the pretension of absoluteness either in thought or dogma, but more pervasively and creatively as the enhancement of meaning, the factor which heightens the value and significance of events or relationships. It is the quality which manifests itself wherever life is actually redeemed from chaos, or a person is enabled to achieve his own destiny with unequivocal certainty. It is only when the end glorifies the means and they become as ends in themselves that we confront the unmistakable "good news," the logos in the world. To witness to that, to proclaim it not as a message but as a demonstration, is our mandate if religion is to contribute anything to the deficiencies of the technical age. Nowhere is the lack more glaring than in the need for moral order in the large-scale structures of new powers and new freedoms.

As one looks back across the pages of this brief excursion, the inadequacy of it is appalling in the light of the rumbling earthquake of our age. We looked briefly at the new shape of things rising like a new continent from the sea of history; we sketched the contour of major claims which such a world requires of religion. But we indicated no means to achieve such ends; we described no technique for manipulating the forces arrayed in the crisis; we suggested no organization, no representative committee, no assembly of delegates, no agency for elaborating a dynamic bureaucracy with far-traveling experts and high-speed mimeographs, and no sociological or demographic or educational survey—in short, it is to be suspected that the problem is of a kind which does not lend itself to the current methods of technical control. It may mean that we shall have to revert to slower and even more unsure ways just to get our hands and hearts on the real problem.

Whatever the turns are likely to be in history, they probably will surprise us. The one sure thing about history is that there is nothing sure about it. What will happen to the church, or to religion, or to faith, in this technical age is hard to say. How can we demonstrate true community of sufficient size and depth as to fit the enormous dimensions of the new society? How can we reactivate the ancient symbols so they can once again embrace the full reconciliation of man's mystery in this diversified and sophisticated age? How can we reassert the lively and exciting recognition of the transcendent in a world of crass contingency, computers, and cheap salesmanship? How can we produce a new kind of person, able to transcend the smug, appearance-loving bourgeoisie, the shrewd go-getter, the big operator, the smooth dilettante, the knowing fop? How can we purge the church of its stupid success mongering, its worship of bigness, its egregious love of safety, its pious inanity?

When Karl Jaspers closed his remarkably perceptive book on *Man in the Modern Age*,[4] he bluntly says, "No definite answer can be given to the question: 'What is going to happen?' Man, living man, will answer this question through his own being, in the course of his own activities. A forecast of the future . . . can aim only at rendering mankind aware of itself." It is this latter phrase which points the way to the only action we can take: namely, to do all in our power to render mankind aware of itself! The church does not need to be

---

[4] Garden City: Doubleday (Anchor ed.), 1957.

numerically large or institutionally a success; it does not need to be respectable or popular, well organized or financially sound, dogmatically self-assured or firmly orthodox, to fulfill its essential destiny in the role of history or in the economy of the world, but it does need to have a passionate understanding of what it means to be a human being, caught between the massive pressures of society and the irreducible hope of the spirit. It is for religion to declare in unmistakable terms, both of insight and of compassion, the sin and the sublimity which constitute our nature as men. In the freedom we cannot escape, try as we will, we must take this world in all its disturbing newness and bewildering size and frightening power, and shape it until at last it manifests our meaning and reflects our purpose. God's will may be not unlike the great angel at the brook Jabbok, where Jacob wrestled with a nameless adversary, till blessed he found himself another man. So we may wrestle through a long night of agony with obscure forces before we break through into a new humanity, blest by the Everlasting.

THE FUNCTION
OF RELIGION

R eligion is both radical and conservative. In its radical form, religion attempts to get underneath the surface of life and discover its meaning. Religion seeks to get at the heart of things; to find the purpose of life and how best to live it. Religion does not believe, any more than science or art, that reality is given, easily found on the surface of life. It is firmly convinced that life's essential meaning must be discovered by a serious discipline and through certain disclosures which occur now and then in the rough circumstances of human existence. One cannot glibly add everything together and make sense. The intimations of life's real significance are revealed only in special occasions when the mind of man is illuminated by a penetrating vision of something beyond the routine. The radical side of religion is hospitable to new experiences; it works to keep men's consciences alive and sensitive. It is open.

On the other hand, religion is conservative. Once it gets a hand on an occasion when the meaning of life is revealed, it tends to hold onto it tenaciously. Indeed, this is quite human simply because the ordinary routine of life seems to have so much less clarity, light, and excitement that one does not want to relinquish the particular form in which the illumination first occurred. Religion, therefore, tends not only to go deep but also to cling to a great many events which originally had considerable meaning, but which in time become rigid and actually a burden to the spirit. These are the two sides of religion which perennially characterize the human experience— one driving us to the deeper levels of existence, the other

Given before Alumni Representatives at Harvard in 1964, and published under the title of "Minister to this Age," in the *Harvard Alumni Bulletin* of February 15, 1964.

tenaciously hanging onto certain past experiences in what sometimes seems a desperate attempt to conserve what has been most revealing in life.

In ancient tradition, the conservative tendency is represented by the priest; the radical attempt to get at the root of things in their newness is represented by the prophet. These two haunt us even today, for there is still tension between the past which has been conserved and the present which is in anguish and tumult. It is the difference between tradition and revolution. Here in the Divinity School we are well aware that we cannot serve the cause of religion or maintain its vitality in the world without reckoning with the radical tendency to go as far into the meaning of existence as we can, or, on the other hand, without conserving, as wisely as we may, those events which have revealed to men a superior wisdom for living.

Once we have accepted this difficult tension as a portion of our responsibility in educating men for the ministry and for teaching, we must take into account a series of revolutions which have shaped our world: revolutions which have thrown a particular burden upon the nature of religious experience, created great bewilderment, and along with it, of course, considerable misunderstanding and disillusionment. Let me enumerate these revolutions rather briefly.

First, out of the Renaissance of three centuries ago the tremendous forces erupted which created the tidal wave of individualism in contemporary life. One can see this wave rising in the sixteenth century as a new impetus to tease the individual out of the mass of the Middle Ages until at last he stood on his own feet, independent, self-reliant. There came into being a whole new image of man—later to become the hero of romanticism. Again, out of the emotional pressures developing the idea of the hero, comes the rebel as an exaggerated form of individualism. In both the individualist and the rebel one confronts a personality-characteristic of our modern age, the difficulty of coming to terms with the communal structures of life. We seem better able to create corporations than communities. So we have great difficulty in handling the normal communal structures of religion. For religion is not essentially an individualistic enterprise. It is a fellowship, a covenant among people who possess a common stock of emotion and feeling, attitude and trust, toward the mysteries of human existence and of God. In our day, this is one of the great tensions between the Biblical structures of meaning and the present realities of man's nature.

Second, the scientific revolution came at the end of the Middle Ages and stimulated the analytical and discursive reason of man. In most instances, it tended to objectify as well as to impersonalize its concern. Science, which has been so successful in probing the mysteries of the world and of nature, bringing us to tremendous progress in so many areas, is also a force that has embarrassed the characteristically symbolic conceptions of religion and made it increasingly difficult to handle the personal participative character of religious life, over against the analytical, critical, and objective forms of scientific methodology.

The third revolution is the industrial, which arose rapidly, spread throughout civilization, and characterizes much of our culture. The industrial has become a mode of life, emphasizing work and evaluating progress in quantitative terms. It is no secret to any of us that values of efficiency, productiveness, speed, quantity, have all become highly emotional and, to a large degree, sanctified as sufficient motivation and satisfaction for our life. Indeed, these norms have now been introduced into the life of the church. Our usual way of evaluating the worth of a religious institution today is to determine how big it is, how many members it has, how fast it grows, how munificent its budget, and how large its staff! Scarcely religious, these criteria have their proper place in industry.

Then there is Sigmund Freud whose clinical explorations added to our world a whole new dimension of life, a fourth revolution. To be sure, men had always had a subconscious, but they did not always know they had one. This new consciousness of the unconscious, recognizing the mechanisms by whose peculiar skulduggery we fool ourselves, is a new, complicating burden to be borne in seeking spiritual peace and security. It has greatly complicated the interpretation of human nature on which theology ultimately must rest its doctrines of redemption and salvation.

In the fifth place, there is the revolution, our most recent, which has accompanied the discovery of atomic fission. Here we have entered into a profound breakthrough in the field of force. We tremble before the magnitude of our discovery and the dread of insufficient moral strength to control what we have in our hands. We dream of space travel. Already we have populated the outer space of our earth with various pieces of hardware. No wonder paranoid hopes have sprung up that spy stations can be set up of such a nature as to control the destiny of men, not only upon our own planet, but anywhere else they may exist.

All these revolutions have conspired to produce a most difficult era in which the radical revelations of the past, rising out of the traditional history of man's penetration into the meaning of life, are threatened and obscured by the equally radical breakthroughs of contemporary science and industry.

To make traditions sound like sense in a world as revolutionary as ours, to light up the past, to bring it into conjunction with the present so that there may be mutual illumination, interpreting the radical experiences of antiquity, to give some guidance to new perspectives and dimensions of life and consciousness in our time—all this provides us with a severe burden as well as an exciting responsibility.

I suppose one of the most perceptive men in our generation studying the cultural problems men face was Robert Oppenheimer, the physicist. In his Columbia University address several years ago, he described the world of our day: its prevalence of newness, its changing scale, the scope of change itself; a world that seems to alter as we walk in it, and the years of man's life to measure not some small growth or rearrangement of what he learned in childhood but to measure a great upheaval. Over against this, Oppenheimer said succinctly, "What is new in this world is the massive character of the dissolution and corruption of authority—in belief, in ritual, and in temporal order. Yet this is the world that we have come to live in." Here is an accurate definition of our problem: "the massive character of the dissolution of authority, in belief, in ritual, and in temporal order." Oppenheimer might have added "in security." For somehow or other, the vast upheavals of the Renaissance, of the scientific revolution, of the industrial changes, of the Freudian psychiatry, of fission, of space travel —all these things have upset our world so markedly that none of us feels very comfortable about the future. Take, for example, the juxtaposition of the great forces that are operating in our world today.

Think for a moment of the population explosion. At one time reproduction could be divinely enjoined upon the human race as the command of God to go forth and multiply and replenish the earth, but now sexual power is as lethal as that of atomic fission. It took 1600 years to double the population of the world, and yet in the next fifty years it will be doubled again. Think of what it means that each four years we shall add to the world a number equal to the population of the United States. Place against this explosion which threatens food supply, stimulates prejudices of angry racists, and produces political paranoia, the fact that we are now, in the United States alone, losing forty thousand jobs weekly, due to automation. As fast as the population is growing, even faster by the techniques of engineering and industry do we deprive men of the privilege of working. Mankind isn't very happy without work. Where will your grandchildren get work to do? Have you thought about it? Will they be forced to endure not merely a two-day yawn each weekend, but five days of unendurable boredom? And, if so, will they escape the kind of ennui that leads to what Jan Masaryk once called Western civilization's greatest crisis; namely, the tendency toward suicide? For suicide is born out of boredom, not out of work; 200,000 people in the United States attempt it each year! In the most prosperous, best entertained, the most distracted, and the most frenzied nation in the world!

Over against the population explosion and automation, consider the peculiar implications of the statement which came from the late President Kennedy when asked about the lethal character of the bombs in our stockpiles. "We could," he said, "kill 300,000,000 in an hour," and then added, "We might even do a little better." The connection this has with the population explosion and the boredom of a world without much work to do is not too hard to see. We cannot think of 300,000,000 people as individual human beings, only as so many units of life, more or less expendable.

Or add again to this the fact that in the last ten years

800,000,000 people have pushed their way out from colonial status to freedom and hot independence. Here is a vast potpourri of extraordinary forces and powers that simply do not seem to be any longer under rational control. We wish they were. We are striving to find our way to control them. But the dread we feel, the insecurity we know, the anxiety which gnaws at us hour by hour, are an indication that the population explosion is not yet manageable, nor are the effects of automation. Neither do we have the moral ability to hold in check the dangerous, paranoid suspicions of nations holding within their grasp enormous amounts of destructive power. Moreover, even if the great nations do manage to achieve sanity and poise, how long will some smaller nation, less responsible, less capable, maintain its poise in the midst of the world's irregular and threatening catastrophes?

There's no doubt about it. Religion has a tremendous task to face today. The minister and the teacher cannot merely repeat the traditions of the past, to conserve only the insights that once were good for the eighth century B.C. or the first century A.D., or the sixteenth century. They must be profoundly concerned both to conserve what is good in the past for the sake of the present and to enter radically into the deepest exploration of the present in order to discern the work of God's hand in the age in which we live.

What does religion have to offer this new world in which the fundamental bases of order have been taken away? I am not suggesting that religion could possibly have results as immediate as a tax cut or a farm subsidy. Religion is too deeply embedded in the foundations, and too intimately derived from the hidden resources, of man's spirit to effect an abrupt change in history. Fundamentally, the function of religion is to supply the world with a structure of symbolism which will articulate, not explain, the mysteries of human existence and give man some inkling of ultimate purpose in life. By such structures as the myth, the rite, and the symbol, man organizes his life, both as an individual and as a member of society. Where the people are able to carry in their minds some vision of what man ought to be and what life can be, they are able to relate themselves to one another in trust and in understanding. By such a relationship, they constitute and sustain the very building of a social order, a community, a society. Wherever people lack this picture of the meaning of existence in symbolic terms, where they do not have a common denominator with one another, where they lose the ability to cohere as a group because their contacts with one another become competitive, rebellious, paranoid, then society disintegrates.

The interesting thing is that any thoroughgoing study of history confirms this rather quick observation which I have made. Werner Jaeger, in his famous work, *Paideia,* traces the transition of Greek democracy from one age to another and indicates that when poetry, music, and religion declined, and the images and symbols of these experiences evaporated from the Greek mind, then the democracy of Greece began to disintegrate. Jan Huizinga, the Dutch scholar, studying the late medieval period, spends considerable time indicating the peculiar way in which the symbolic life of that age went to seed. As the symbols grew less and less meaningful, as they were elaborated in more and more artificial ways, when at last they began to disappear, then the Middle Ages lost political, communal, and social structure. Lewis Mumford has put the matter very briefly in one of his Bamford Lectures at Columbia: When a people collapse, it is not because of famine or economic failure within, or military attack from without, but always because the symbolic structures have become dislocated.

Surely this is what Robert Oppenheimer meant by "the dissolution and corruption of authority—in belief, in ritual, and in temporal order." Ultimately, no society can hold itself together unless it has some kind of symbolism to sustain it. This is what concerns the whole discipline of theological education. We are trying here to introduce men to those more radical and profound aspects of religious symbolism which have the power to embrace the tensions of this world and its contradictions and hold them in some kind of meaningful unity. We do not pretend that rituals of thought or of action or of devotion are in any sense explanations. We are trying to say that life cannot be lived abundantly, either for the individual or for society as a whole, without some device of symbolism which has the power to bring together into meaningful tensions the extraordinary mysteries of man's many-sided relationships and his multileveled experience. Religion, without being pretentious, seeks somehow to be the common bond that brings together art and science, philosophy and economics, politics and industry; to establish among them all a correlation in which man's full being may be expressed in dignity and in the hope of his proper destiny.

Our theological training is trying to keep alive in a technological world all those feelings which tend to be obliterated, or obscured, or smothered. We believe most devoutly in man and in his possibilities as one capable, under God's grace, of recovering the meaning of life and fulfilling it. But mankind is threatened by the very success of the revolutions through which he has passed: the rise of the individual and his final denouement as a kind of rebel against everything, which characterizes portions at least of our contemporary culture; the rise of the scientific attitude which tends to absolutize the impersonal and the objective; the rise of the industrial revolution, in which life is commercialized; the Freudian revolution in which we are confronted by the demonic forces that seem to deceive us, trick us, manipulate us at unmanageable levels of our being; the dreadful nuclear power which we hold in our unsteady hands. These great revolutions, these huge successes, now bring us to the point where the human center is threatened by a world which man himself has made; threatened by forces he has released; threatened by systems over which he seems to have little control; threatened indeed by the very depths of man's own demonic self.

We are still seeking to find in religion a radical penetration to the meaning of life and equally to protect a tradition in relation to the continued conviction that man must be conserved in the total magnitude of his being. We cannot afford to reduce the mystery of man, his need, his manifold nature, one slight bit, for it is on him that the burden of the world's peace depends. Here at Harvard we are training ministers and teachers with the most deliberate effort to produce men with professional competence in the full conservation of those experiences and qualities, those occasions and revelations of the past, which have meaning in the establishment of a firm world for our present era. But while we are teaching men to interpret the Bible with sanity and intelligence and the theological tradition we have inherited, we also believe that this alone is not enough. These men must also have the power of dynamic leadership in discriminately reshaping the contemporary world of revolution in ways that will provide men with a stable society and a meaningful existence. They must have a perceptive awareness, not only of the religious world of the past, but of that renaissance of religion in the arts and in the business and politics of our own day. Their eyes must be keen to see the present world as the kingdom in which God is now moving, as well as to see the historical perspective in which God has moved in ages past. The long disciplines of preparation must give them wisdom and compassion for the superb chance to minister to this age with its troubles and its triumphs.

RELIGION: HEALTHY
AND UNHEALTHY

When Alexis de Tocqueville, a hundred and fifty years ago, observed the American scene with such perceptive eyes, he declared that nowhere had he seen so much lunacy in religion as in America. Certainly in the beginning America was as violent in its religious behavior as it was in most other aspects of life. Now that the continent has been conquered and the frontier has disappeared (at least in its geographical sense), one may wonder what De Tocqueville would say to the kind of religion to be found in the quiescent respectability of the contemporary church. Adjustments have been made; compromises between holy zeal and worldly wisdom have been effected; a general refinement and acculturation have smoothed over the jagged conflicts. That the power and intensity of religion have suffered a considerable diminution can scarcely be argued, and that there has occurred an increasing conformity to the social mores of an extra-Christian derivation is equally plain. In that sense, American religion is less lunatic and perhaps more normative; but its creative influence in the large affairs of society remains much in doubt.

To distinguish between healthy and unhealthy religion is extremely difficult. It would be too easy to do it in such a way as to rule out the disturbing geniuses who were the very founders of the great religions. It would be easy to draw the line and unwittingly exclude the great prophets or the outstanding saints. Even in the medical sphere, health is a notoriously difficult state to define. In religion, it is more subtly fraught with problems than in medicine or psychiatry. That

Given before the Academy of Religion and Mental Health, New York, and published in the *Journal of Religion and Health*, July 1965.

Freud, the father of all clinical judgment about man's mental behavior, declared religion to be a universal neurosis has led many of his followers to the not altogether logical conclusion that religion itself was unhealthy, a sign of unreality, and a factor to be eradicated from the psyche, if the person was to become strictly sane. It has been generally forgotten that Freud also said, "Man's superiority over other animals is his capacity for neurosis." Any attempt to separate man from this neurotic capacity simply does not leave us man at all. Man is what he is by reason of his essential neurotic relationship to himself and his world. He is not neurotic accidentally, but intrinsically. His neurosis is not a deviation from his nature, but part and parcel of it, running through it and characterizing the very substance of it. To put the matter in its sharpest paradox, perhaps the most significant sign of a healthy religion is precisely the result of this basic neurotic capacity, which constitutes man's superiority over the brutes.

Some time ago, in an article in *The Atlantic Monthly*, Professor Donald Fleming referred to this fundamental condition. He pointed out that Freud "assimilated the gross neuroses to the strategies of concealment shown to be at work among normal people . . . It did not follow (however) by Freud's lights that everybody was ill, but all life strategies were laid out along a continuous spectrum of deceptions great and small, signifying some degree of aversion from reality. 'Every one of us,' he said, 'behaves in some one respect like a paranoiac, corrects some aspect of the world which is unbearable to him by the construction of a wish and introduces this delusion into reality.' He added that 'delusional remolding of reality' by a number of people in common was the essence of religion." [1] The data, thus given, I must hasten to add, may be read in quite another way.

[1] Donald Fleming. "The Meaning of Mental Illness," *The Atlantic Monthly*, 214:72–76 (1964).

One must ask how the terms "neurotic" and "reality" are being used. To speak of the neurotic as a scientific term, describing the peculiarity of man's relation to himself, or as the peculiarity of man's ability to change the meaning of external events, may be one thing. To use it pejoratively as do Mannheim and Nietzsche, as descriptive of man's sickness, is another. Moreover, to speak of reality as a fixed "given," as if it were the objective nonhuman world, is strangely restrictive. What man creates for himself may be as much a part of reality as what has been created for him. Is a violin less real than wood or catgut in their original separate states? Is the grandeur of Chartres not real because it was not evident in the quarry from which the stone was dug?

The total reality in which man operates as a human being is larger than the law by which his physical nature is conditioned. It is larger than any single aspect of his many-leveled being. His "neurotic capacity," as Freud calls it, is derived precisely from the freedom that is ascribed to him as a child of God. He is not limited to conformity to a fixed reality. His reality is so large and so complex that freedom is the only adequate term for it. Indeed, by such freedom he shares in the creation, shaping it, transforming it, and fulfilling it. By the plastic power of his perception and activity, and such resources of responsibility, he transforms the nature of the objective world and elicits its meaning. This is the place where religion, healthy or unhealthy, operates.

When we turn, then, to ask how religion engages in this total reality, we affirm two things about it. First, it penetrates the events that constitute the circumstantial levels of our life and affirms within and beyond them a mystery that can be trusted without being comprehended. Second, it thinks of reality as something in which man, in his total being, and the world are fulfilled together.

If we were to put these two things together, we would describe religion as a structure of symbols, myths, and rites by which the mysteries of human existence are articulated, from which both society and the individual derive a common base of value and meaning. This symbolic structure is embedded in concrete events, which are assumed to have universal relevance. Such mysteries of man's life—sin, death, sex, shame— are articulated without being explained. That is to say, the essential contradictions of life and death, good and evil, freedom and necessity, are in no sense abrogated or repudiated. They are formulated, not logically or rationally, but in the only way they can be, namely, in the capacious symbol where the singular and the universal may both be affirmed, and where contrariety may exist interdependently. It is this concrete universal or intensive compressive, as Cassirer speaks of it, that forms the common base for the coherence of society and the security of the individual.

Without such a base of images, society loses its cohesiveness and tends to disintegrate, while the individual fails to get the support he needs for the exercise of his freedom. I am inclined to believe that there can be no society without such a symbolic structure. Held in the mind of its members and practiced in cultic remembrance, it is the source of social community and the ground of individual integrity. A healthy religion provides such a structure. Where faith reverts to divisive sectarianism, incapable of broad unities, or, even worse, to private individualism, it contributes to the sickness and deterioration of society.

This is precisely our present embarrassment, that in a world where the symbolic formulary of religion has been progressively diminished over the last three centuries by a highly rationalistic emphasis, the social cohesion of the world has been greatly lessened; so much so that society resorts to all kinds of coercive methods—fascist, nazi, marxist, and just plain committees—to maintain a semblance of order. Moreover, our attempt to find a coherent and unifying force in technology, which would provide us with the symbols sufficiently dynamic and human to sustain a sane and healthy society, has proved futile. Technology simply does not have within itself images appropriate for the essentially human, for its breadth and depth, its contradictions and subtlety, its complexity and perversity of experiences common to man. The image of the machine, or of atoms, or of causality, are all too narrow, too shallow, and too metallic.

A healthy religion, then, will provide us with a structure of imaginative unity, a picture of the whole, without in the least diminishing the inner tensions and obvious contradictions. It will be an intuitive unity, replete with its own mystery, unprovable but thoroughly empirical. It does not deny doubts or erase conflict, or even avoid tragedy. From the formulary of images it derives a set of values by which the community fashions its mores, its tastes, its sense of sanctity and sin. And by these it imposes on the phantasmagoria of history and the irregularities of human impulse a style of behavior.

A healthy religion is not a science; that is to say, it is not a description of an external reality. It is a symbolism, projected from within reality, from within total reality, by which man adroitly and indirectly handles the provocative mystery of human existence, which he cannot directly discern or literally describe. Even in the natural sciences we have begun to realize that reality cannot be reduced to the simple category of objectivity.

There are two questions that must be asked at this point. First, is it neurotic for man, caught in the stream of existence to make an effort to reach some idea about the nature of the whole? All men do! Even those who jump to the conclusion that the whole conglomeration of things—stars and cabbages and kings—makes no sense at all. If it is neurotic to make such a guess, by faith positive, by doubt negative, should we not say that anything as universal as this is normative for human beings? Should we say "normatively neurotic"? What, then, should we say of those persons who refuse to share in the universal trait and seek a neutral stance? Is it healthier to be Melville's Ahab or Camus' Meurseault, a man angrily engaged in thrusting his fist through the masks to find out the meaning of things, or a man utterly indifferent, one who could not care less?

The second question is whether we can separate the religious structure that sustains the sanity of both society and the individual from those demonic forces that incessantly prey upon faith to divert it to unhealthy perversions and superstitions.

Here, it seems to me, one can see why the religious structure is so often and so easily perverted. It operates in the realm of freedom, at the level where images and symbols, rites and myths, are shaped out of infinite diversity and with energies from every dimension of human life. It does not take much to turn or twist these intentions a hair's breadth at one point and to find the end of the line grotesquely askew. There is no structure of faith that has not been thus misread or abused. The rule of discipline, pushed too far, has eventuated in masochistic flagellation; undue anxiety produces scrupulosity; fear twists God into a devil; pride of orthodoxy produces sadism; paranoid suspicion creates heresy hunters. History, both ancient and recent, is full of examples, both of individuals and of whole communities or sects, who managed to turn the structure of religion from reality to uses of compensation and extreme aberration.

In contrast, the essential aspect of a healthy religion is its ability to remain in relation to the threatening aspects of reality without succumbing to fear, shame, anxiety, or hostility.

The symbolic structure of all religions is built around the re-curring traumata of human existence. The fear of ultimate reality or of God, the abyss of annihilation or nothingness, the shattering sense of shame, the overwhelming power of sex—all these experiences are sacramentalized in religion. The un-canny, the awesome, the uncontrollable, the holy, the ecstatic —all are accommodated, domesticated, sanctified within the sacraments. They are made acceptable; they become bearable. In a healthy religion, the relationship to reality, that is, to death, to sex, to shame, is maintained. It is part of sanity to know how both to fear and not to fear, to be related but not to be absorbed, to face flux but not to be lost in it. An un-healthy religion runs away, becomes obsessed with a part in order to avoid the whole.

There are many ways to illustrate this condition. A religion that fears the subconscious tries to live entirely on the rational level and piously announces its intellectual superiority. An-other sect eschews the rational and wallows in the masturba-tion of the emotions. Still another denies the reality of pain and evil in the name of an abstract perfection. The body is denied for the soul's sake; the flexible future becomes more fascinating than the inflexible present; all truth is rigidly lim-ited to the Bible. The synoptic vision of healthy faith is thus lost for the one-eyed fanaticism of unhealthy perversions.

It must be confessed that modern religion, particularly in its Protestant form, is especially lacking in the vigor and depth of its symbolic structures. By its iconoclasm over the last three centuries, it has deprived itself of the most dynamic asset of religion, namely, its visual and liturgical suggestiveness. In-stead, it has relied almost entirely on verbal communication, an indication of its excessive rationalism. Roman Catholicism and Greek orthodoxy, by contrast, have maintained their sym-bolism, but, unfortunately, have failed to revise it in terms of contemporary experience. A rational religion, by its very terms, is an incomplete religion, reducing the total spectrum of reality by excluding references to the subconscious dynamics where images control energies and ideas are relatively impotent. But, on the other hand, the revolutions in the rational presuppositions of the way in which we understand the world and self cannot be excluded from the religious symbols without emasculating their force.

It is not strange that religion has been weakened by this process, for the whole culture has deprived itself of a healthy symbolism. What there is exists largely in its vulgarized commercial form in advertising.

This brings me to a last question. What is the shape and stance of a healthy religion in a neurotic culture? One can scarcely miss the impact of this culture on all classes, from children through youth to old age—its frenetic compulsiveness, its excessive mobility, its accelerated acceleration, its incessant change, its lack of fixed forms, its fragmentation, its spurious values, its mania for violence, and at the same time its dependence on tranquilizers. Nowhere is the essential quality of the shift seen more vividly than in the elevation of the industrial mores in place of the traditional religious values. All the hyperaggressive virtues, spawned by the Industrial Revolution and the rise of the bourgeoisie, have been substituted for the inner disciplines of the classical Christian beatitudes. The middle class, in which these revolutions centered, now seems interested, as Berdyaev put it, more in appearance than in being. Prestige, success, ambition, conspicuous consumption, all take precedence as motivations for the new age. Respectability was mistaken for righteousness. Even the church lost its understanding of the meaning of the spirit, and worked for success, measured in statistical and institutional terms.

To adjust to such a culture is itself to open oneself to an

essentially abnormal life. To react against it is usually accounted neurotic. But perhaps the only way to be humanly and religiously normal is to be neurotic in our deviation from the culture now regnant.

In conclusion, religion is healthy if it provides us with a sufficiently rich and suggestive symbolic structure, not to explain life but to articulate its mysteries in such a way as to provide society with a common base of feeling and the individual with a vision of his most intimate and ineluctable experiences as a human being. In its rites it should enable a man to remember the elusive dimensions and qualities of his being, and to recover them by liturgical action. It should keep man close to and open toward powerful forces hidden in the psyche, without rendering him subject to their naked threat, for this is the source of most of his vitality and sense of life. It should embrace both the rational and subconscious levels of the self, both the power of existence and the meaning of it. It should relate past with present, myth with reality, symbol with existence. A healthy religion unites existence; an unhealthy one divides it.

RIVETS AND
REALITY

In Joseph Conrad's story "Heart of Darkness" there is an unforgettable scene when the river steamer is held up for repairs and Marlow is driven to desperation in his effort to find the necessary materials to do the job. Africa with its teeming, murky life; its frenzied howling natives dancing on the banks, and then by contrast its mysterious stillness and languor, rise up to tempt and taunt the captain. Technical efficiency, the world of Europe, is stranded at the very edge of the jungle, the primitive darkness. With a deliberate stubbornness of will, Marlow busies himself at the repairs, as he says because "in that way only it seemed . . . I could keep my hold on the redeeming facts of life." But what Marlow needed most was rivets.

"What I really wanted," he said, "was rivets, by Heaven! Rivets." To get on with the work—to stop the hole. Rivets I wanted. There were cases of them down at the coast—cases —piled up—burst—split! You kicked a loose rivet at every second step in that station yard on the hillside. Rivets had rolled into the grove of death. You could fill your pockets with rivets for the trouble of stooping down—and there wasn't one rivet to be found where it was wanted. *We had plates that would do, but nothing to fasten them with.*

Weeks pass by in the awful stalemate, and something of symbolic significance becomes evident when Marlow exclaims "What I wanted was rivets—and really rivets was what Mr. Kurtz wanted, if he had only known it."

The gist of this remark is that neither Marlow nor Kurtz was able to hold things together, a condition which Yeats had described as all coherence gone—the center no longer

Given at St. Olaf College, Northfield, Minnesota, in June 1962.

holds—things fall apart—the ritual of innocence is lost. Marlow, by heavy-handed, feverish restraint, can turn his back on the primitive by tinkering with technology, while Kurtz, whose mind flashes out in vast visions of an ultimate Utopia, falls prey to the "horror" near at hand. Rivets—something to hold the world together—is what we all need. What frustrates us is the knowledge that there are, or were, rivets elsewhere. Other ages, other cultures—other people—who knew some secret we have lost, by which they saw life steadily and saw it whole, these we cannot forget, though we may be tempted to deny.

There are two sides to this basic question: the public side—how do we hold the world together, and the private side—how do we keep the self together. I take it that education which is not concerned with such an issue is scarcely worthy of the name. It is in a broad and very serious sense the moral responsibility of education to be concerned precisely with the integrity of the individual, and at one and the same time quite inevitably with the nature of reality by which the world is sustained in some degree of meaning and unity.

Something of the problem which Marlow faced in his need for rivets is seen in the prophetic glimpse of Dostoevsky's little man who crawled out from under the floor boards in *Letters from the Underworld*. You will remember he found a very efficient world, very scientific and technological, a kind of crystal palace established with all kinds of protections, securities, justices. "I should not be surprised," says Dostoevsky, "if amid all the order and regularity of the future, there should suddenly arise, from some quarter or another, some gentleman of lowborn—or rather, of retrograde and cynical—demeanour who, setting his arms akimbo, should say to you all: 'How now, gentlemen? Would it not be a good thing, if, with one consent, we were to kick all this solemn wisdom to the winds, and to send those logarithms to the devil, and to begin to live our lives again according to our own stupid whims?' Yet this would be as nothing; the really shameful business would be that this gentleman would find a goodly number of adherents."

Here again rivets are needed. How can this vastly elaborated, frighteningly expanding crystal palace of technology, motivated by the pure chrome steel motives of science, be firmly attached to the human world—that gross, wayward, perverse, erratic world of flesh and dreams, dust and destiny, will and whim? What rivets shall be required to bind together the plates of man and society, of flesh and the machine; of the heart's darkness and reason's cold, blundering light, of faith and fact, of poetry and planning, of freedom and order, of things and the spirit? Or will we be stranded with our high-priced technical wonders at the edge of the jungle—tempted, tormented, taunted by dreams we cannot satisfy and a height and depth we dare not admit while we tinker at the small repairs, for want of rivets—rivets to hold the world together, meaningfully, magnificently? What impasse will we reach by the horizontal elaboration of a vast web of shining technological devices for transportation and communication if this electronic civilization has no deep foundations in the human order?

One remembers Ahab in "Moby Dick" musing "Hark ye yet again—the little lower layer. All visible objects, man, are but as pasteboard masks. But in each event—as the living act, the undoubted deed—there, some unknown but still reasoning thing puts forth the mouldings of its features from behind the unreasoning mask. If man will strike, strike through the mask." But how do we reach this "little lower level," break through the superficial mask, come face to face with reality? This is the moral issue raised by education at its most serious.

Let us put the matter metaphorically. Where does education need rivets? I should like to suggest that one of the grave tendencies in present education is the reduction of the college to a warehouse of ideas—ideas of every sort and kind, stored neatly in thousands of carefully labeled bins, departmentalized, jargonized, sorted and re-sorted by meticulous research, always available for new combinations or even descriptions, unnumbered, catalogued, classified, programmed, and well cleansed as usable data on any research assembly line. Indeed, one of the destructive accomplishments of the culture in which we live is its marked ideological character. That is to say, it is strikingly ideological in contrast to previous epochs by reason of the primal importance we give to ideas. They are our very life and substance. We don't know how to approach anything directly; we have to have an idea of it, and through the idea we handle it, so to speak. We have a lust for ideas. They are as ubiquitous and often as fantastic and as far removed from reality as the lush, lunatic symbolism of the Middle Ages. Because there is little contact with the restraints of reality, they grow like parasites, airborne, hanging in the air. The generic name for this kind of thing, I suppose, is sophistication. The best description of it is in De Tocqueville's observations of American Democracy, where he says that we "are constantly finding it necessary to rely upon ideas (we) have not had time to explore thoroughly; men are led to attach an excessive value to the rapid bursts and superficial conceptions of the intellect, and on the other hand to undervalue unduly its slower and deeper labors."

There are several consequences of this mass consumption of ideas. Beyond the fact that there is an assumption that many ideas make a wise man, and the profligacy of public opinions is taken to mean some kind of private conviction—both false of course—there is a kind of tumbleweed instability about it. Ideas need to be riveted to something; otherwise they float off in any direction at the slightest gust of wind to rationalize the most outrageous passions, public or private. In a recent discussion, President Millicent MacIntosh of Barnard College is reported to have said that it was Germany who encouraged its graduate students "to move rapidly and directly into areas of specialized knowledge." "But," she continued, "if those German students had had the opportunity in which they might reflect upon their knowledge, upon the world, upon themselves, and upon their human responsibilities, then perhaps the recent history of our world might have been very different."

One must ask ultimately whether reality dwells in the head or in the whole man, and if in the whole man, then education must reckon with larger dimensions if it is to prove responsible.

Let me put the matter strongly. An unlimited development of sheer ideas, unbalanced by other factors in man's self, can lead as quickly to idiocy as any vulgar sin of the flesh. Indeed the peculiar hell of our epoch may be precisely that which is inherent in the accumulation of infinite facts without meaning —in short, a sophisticated hell, intellectually brilliant but existentially in despair. A phrase of Karl Jasper's which he in turn draws from Nietzsche—"the nihilism of strength"—applies here. Our biggest asset may be overtaken by its own nemesis. It is highly possible that if there were fewer ideas, and these deeply rooted, man would be more intelligent in handling himself and his world. A remark of Ezra Pound's, which has long remained with me, is, that it is not the number of ideas a man holds which marks a man, but the depth at which he holds them.

It may be precisely this lack of depth which may provide a key for leading us beyond the sorry state of shoring up the ruins with the pitiful fragments of our exploded world. There are three aspects of the same direction which would open the question up at another level. Perhaps the first of these is the simplest and most obvious inability to pull our world together meaningfully. There are rivets in one place, and a battered ship a hundred miles away; there are all kinds of unitary principles, here, there, and elsewhere, political and scientific, but the schisms which rend our world are too deep and broad to be pulled together by abstract formulas or superficial slogans.

Certainly the most obvious need for rivets, so to speak, in the educational process is at the point where the very freedom of inquiry becomes chaos and works against itself in the final outcome of producing a wise person. Instead there comes forth a man with a honeycombed, pigeon-holed brain, with a set of rigid terms and facts stuck here and there according to the course labels in which he discovered them. There is neither common ground nor continuity nor coherence among them. Each section has its own authorities and its own sacrosanct vocabulary. Every precaution is taken to prevent a leak —either methodologically or substantively—from one compartment to another. Each department has its own basic kerygma which must not be confused with another.

It is not merely pluralistic in the Jamesian sense; it is schizophrenic in the Freudian sense. It denies what we know to be basically true, namely, that everything that exists depends on an infinite number of relationships which form a vast sustaining web of meaning.

Or turn to C. R. Collingwood's analysis of the split-up of the psyche of man at the end of the Middle Ages. The destructive energies which had been held in the thrall of medieval unity broke asunder, so that the aesthetic sense was no longer dominated by religious themes; the political sense likewise threw off religious constraints; the discursive reason developed science and repudiated any authority but truth considered objectively. This development within man was quickly manifested in the exterior world by autonomous vocations and self-conscious activities in the realm of art, government, and science. Each sphere stood in rebellion against the unity that had traditionally bound all together in a religious whole. Church and state were now carefully set apart; the artist and the saint went their separate ways, developing a high degree of suspicion of each other; and the scientist and the ecclesiastic began a long battle of endless controversies. After three or four centuries of such a development, both within man's consciousness and in his cultural activity, we now stand at the point where we are unable to identify for the most part the religious factors in the political sphere of government; nor are we able to express our religious experience in the aesthetic mode of visual symbols or myths; nor do we know how to recover the religious implications of a scientifically objectified nature. We are split, schizophrenically divided, holding within ourselves and our world several competing, perhaps contradictory, exclusively inclined fragments, each boisterously claiming to be the whole, or at least the highest.

What we have now, both within ourselves and outside in the world, is a riot of specialized segments of experience, literally unable to understand the others, suspicious and arrogant, each trying to prove itself superior and woefully bereft of the sustaining assistance of the whole of life. The religious is serious enough but lacks art for the expression and communication of its meaning; art is in a perfect tumult because it is separated from religion and lacks depth; politics, always concerned with social order, failing to find assistance in depth from religion or in breadth from art, tends to be coercive and fanatical, drifting easily into one form or another of tyranny in its effort to make order and unity when there is none. Morally lacking the seriousness of depth, and the comprehensiveness of breadth, we all become impoverished and lack the strength to create community, and in our failure desperately struggle to organize by technical means the vast collectivities of cities as a compensation.

I am not pleading for medieval unity, or for an external and artificial imposition of unity, or even for a kind of impossible, Utopian homogeneity. Far from it. We cannot use the framework of ancient Greece or the medieval vision of Dante, however great they were. It is our inescapable responsibility to achieve our own vision at a time when it seems almost impossible to stretch our imagination far enough to embrace such extreme and desperate points of view. What I believe may still be possible is such a recovery of man's basic integrity, a new sense of his essential unity, that education may pay more attention to putting a man together than with filling him up with ill-assorted varieties of mutually hostile *Weltanschauungs*.

If teachers can achieve some degree of synoptic vision, and students can be led toward a goal and not toward a degree, then there is still a chance in this most diversified of all cultures that we may be able to recover direction so as to have a purpose, and to glimpse at least some kind of unity so as to have meaning. Without this, all the king's horses and all of Teller's nuclear bombs, all the economic wealth and engineering know-how of America, will not keep us and our world from falling into pieces. We need rivets—large ones, and strong.

Let us turn again to the level at which man holds such ideas as education may furnish. Where can we find rivets to bind together the loose pieces of information and the basic design of a man's life? How do we manage to root ideas so that they are something more than tumbleweed? How can we bind ideas to profound feelings? Only when we can reach into that dark but powerful realm of human passion that lies mysteriously out of reach of reason will we manage to give weight and gravity to our ideas. Only then do they achieve third-dimensional substantiality.

Eric Heller, in *The Hazard of Modern Poetry*[1] has remarked:

The workshops in which our truths are manufactured are surrounded by swarms of unemployed affections. Unemployment leads to riots, and riots there were and are. The most powerful among them in the recent history of thought was romanticism.

But the rub comes when we ask how education may train the feelings, discipline the sensibilities, and root ideas in the firm ground of conviction. Plainly one of the flaws which allows the prolific and irresponsible generation of ideas is that one idea may be engendered from another, without reference to reality. This arbitrary chess game may go on endlessly, producing a world of ghostly abstractions, quite impotent and

[1] Cambridge, England: Bowes & Bowes, 1953, p. 20.

thoroughly deceptive, inhabited by haughty and condescending pedants. One remembers St.Augustine as he is described by C. C. Martindale, S.J., in "A Sketch of the Life and Character of St. Augustine": "Augustine could hold no mere frozen idea before his mind—the thing palpitated forthwith and came to life and he hated it or loved it. If there was intellect in his mysticism, there was passion in his philosophy." [2]

Sigfried Giedion has put the matter succinctly—"Thinking is trained; feeling is left untrained . . . Knowledge and feeling are isolated from each other. So we arrive at the curious paradox that in our period feeling has become more difficult than thinking." Here we must say plainly and unmistakably that any direct manipulation of the feelings is obviously not only wrong but immoral. It is this divorce of idea from feelings, education from sensibility, which is in itself highly suspect if the individual is to achieve integrity. A collection of ideas— no matter how vast—without roots in feeling sooner or later proves sterile and fleeting, usually about six months after graduation. This indeed is why a college education is very temporary for too large a number of students.

There is a very significant negative observation to make in this area of our perplexity, and that is that there is no direct approach to feeling. Feelings are not trained by manipulating feelings; they are the result of the fulfillment of two conditions—first, a respect for the whole person, and second, a distinction between ideas that are engendered by ideas and those which are the articulation of experience itself.

Where there is a whole person, idea and feeling are naturally associated. Where experience moves by reflection into an idea, there is also feeling. In education, then, as in religion, our attention should never be on feeling primarily; that would be quite immoral in the deepest sense of the term. Instead, our attention should be on ideas as the illumination of life, both

[2] Martindale *et al., St. Augustine: His Age, Life and Thought* (New York: Meridian Books, 1957), chap. ii.

with respect to the individual's total existence and to the elucidation of experience. A sort of separate stock-in-trade of ideas is artificial and deceptive.

This brings me to a third need for rivets, for creating a binding integrity in the life of the educated man or woman.

It can be seen if we extend the training of feeling a little further into the region where the choice of excellence is made. How do we train the judgment so that excellence becomes a deliberate and discriminating power in the student? Without that, obviously education is a strange anomaly to say the least. And yet, how can we do it?

I presume in the last analysis the answer is twofold: first by exposure to excellence, and secondly by testifying to such excellence in the very nature of the community itself as well as in explicit apologies in its behalf. By what enthusiasms are students in a particular college motivated? For the most part, a great number of colleges in America are slightly but not much better than high schools. The level of mature consensus, the excellences of masterpieces, either in art or music or philosophy, are lacking. Excellence tends to be a matter of grades, not of objective realities.

Do you remember in *The Catcher in the Rye*, where Holden, having been kicked out of school again, sits on the edge of his sister's bed and talks to her? Phoebe asks him if there is anything he really likes! Likes a lot! He doesn't find it easy to answer. But in him there are answers, and they are quite real, and unfortunately they didn't come out of education. But that is the question which finally comes around to test us more deeply than Rorschach or aptitude tests—What do you like a lot?

You can see plainly what I have been trying to do. I started by saying that we needed rivets to tie together our curriculum, not for its intrinsic or theoretical coordination, but within a man so that he could be assured of his integrity, not by subtracting one aspect of life from all others, and trying to find satisfaction of his many-leveled consciousness in that one alone, but by learning how to be a whole person, alive at every level. Secondly, I pushed into the depth where man feels and feels deeply, where he is himself involved, where things mean something to him, and he either fights them or defends them. This is where truth recovers its motivating power, its satisfying joy. It is no longer a tumbleweed, a loose opinion drifting over desert roads. Finally I reached the question of intimate judgment, namely, what do I count excellent, and worthy of my loyalty?

If I were to characterize this kind of a college, I would say that it deliberately strives by imagination and insight to emulate an open world, a world where all levels of life and all sections of knowledge open out on each other. There simply are no walls except those we erect by arbitrary sign language and private prejudice. It is open between science and religion, between religion and the arts, between the arts and industry. It is open between intelligence and sensibility, between reason and faith, between idea and feeling. It is open between the past and the present, between tradition and revolution, between the classic and the contemporary. It doesn't come to us, naturally or culturally all one, but it does have the possibility of becoming one in the imagination and integrity of man.

THE CHURCH IN A
CHANGING WORLD

A few years ago, Henry Steele Commager of Columbia, the distinguished historian, wrote an article for one of our national magazines, in which he listed the ten most influential factors affecting the life of our times. A reader asked in a somewhat shocked letter why he had omitted religion from the list. Commager's reply was courteous, but crisp. He said he saw no evidence that religion would play a significant role now or in the near future in the revolutionary changes occurring in the world.

If this is true (and there is a great deal to be said in behalf of it), then it is all the more astonishing in the light of the amount of space that religion takes up in the world. Think of its institutional bulk spread all over the world and penetrating every village, every clearing, every island! Think of the incredible mass of its activities, its meetings, and its public and private practices! Think of its unlimited resources of wealth, both in money and in devotees! Think of its hold on the conscience and the fears and the aspirations of the human heart! Add it all up, and then say again that such a staggering accumulation of human activity and concern will not affect the contemporary revolution in our time. It does seem strange, and a bit ironical. And yet I believe Commager is right. Religion in general, as it stands today, is not to be taken seriously in effecting any major change in the life of our time.

Yet, having said this, there is a further irony involved. The changes which distinguish the character of our contemporary

Given at the Rockefeller Memorial Chapel, University of Chicago, on the occasion of the installation of the Reverend E. Spencer Parsons, October 17, 1965.

revolution have all come out of religion—sometimes, it must be confessed, in spite of itself. As Carl von Weizsächer points out in his Gifford Lectures, the very ambiguity of our scientific and secular achievements has derived from their theological and religious origins. Religion has generated a startling and uncomfortable transformation in the consciousness of Western man. The change is more far-reaching than religion itself could have foreseen, and even now strikes religion as a most disturbing and upsetting development. As many a parent looks on his child with astonishment and even resentment, so religion, seeing the secular independence which arose from its own reforms, is tempted to retreat and hold up its hands in shocked dismay. The secular man today—and we are all secular men to the degree we admit we live in the twentieth century—is an embarrassment to the faith which produced him.

This confusion is complex and profound. We are more comfortable, but less contented; healthier physically, but more anxious mentally. We have been liberated from some things, but enslaved to others. Our mobility has increased, but our social stability has been impaired. Our power and control over things has escalated, but we feel uneasy, and we fear the future.

The question we must ask is whether the salt that has lost its savor can be renewed, or must we cast it out to be trodden under foot, under the disgusted and desperate feet of men? Can this fig tree, of such enormous dimensions, but no longer significantly fruitful, be pruned and rendered fruitful for the vital hungers of our time? What kind of reformation is now necessary if the force of faith is to be recovered?

I presume there is little we can do until we recognize that in a world as radically changed in its thought and life, in its perspectives and habits of action, religion itself must change.

To assume that it can remain unchanged and still minister to
the new age, is simply against every evidence of its own history. Religion is not a static deal made once and delivered to
the saints and thereafter passed to succeeding generations, but
a continuing revelation in which history is freshly articulated
in terms of maximum meaning and ultimate destiny. The primordial truths are refashioned, the forms refilled, the rites re-
enacted, the symbols rehabilitated, the faith re-expressed.
Each age, with all its distinct and often embarrassing elements, must find its way to its religious meaning and fulfillment.
Our age is no exception. The changes wrought by philosophy
and science in our notions of reality, the new dimensions of
man's nature, the growing perspectives of society, the shift of
living to technical and urban patterns, the subtle but plain
manifestations of those sensibilities expressed in the arts, the
tempo and mobility of our life—all these and more must rise
at last to play their part and take their place in the religious
vision. That they seem so often recalcitrant and stubborn in
our effort to elicit from them a sign of their divine commission
may be as much an indication of our blindness and perversity
as of their antagonism!

I certainly do not mean by this that all that happens in this
revolutionary world has God's mark of favor on it, and that
we must therefore submit to it. Like Jacob, we must struggle
with this angel of time and place, through much obscurity and
pain, before the blessing is given, and even then we may find
ourselves unable to run as other men. Our problem is that
there is no simple standard to follow, no unqualified *imitatio
Christi* for any age. History itself is too powerful to submit to
a facile application of so-called norms. We confront a seriously
altered environment with a seriously altered heritage, and we
must find our way and a deeper, more candid, honesty than

has been our wont. Meaning—and it is for this we are seeking —is not to be dredged out of the past and plastered on the present. There is a vital dialectic here which we have too often neglected. As damaging as the great schism between Roman Catholicism and Protestantism in the sixteenth century was, faith suffered a more severe impairment in the hidden schism which separated the so-called sacred origins from the secular world. That divorce still paralyzes the fruitful vitality of faith.

Our task is not to prove that God was in the first century, but that he *is* in the twentieth. If men find him now, amid the technological milieu of newsprint, rockets, and H-bombs, they may find him more easily in the reports from the past. The urgency of uncovering a purpose and meaning amid the distractions of overproduction and obsessive speed, in the midst of diffused anxiety and devitalized success, rests heavily upon us.

There are four urgent needs for religious change if faith is to express itself vitally in our time. It must first establish a moral order for human life at a new level of freedom and sophistication; secondly, it must elicit from the present world a new sense of that mystery by which life has been and still is sanctified; thirdly, it must indulge itself in bolder images of faith, in striking syntheses, and in vital liturgies by which man may help to create the unity he hopes to find; and, finally, in all these actions, faith must give birth to a compassion unqualified by its traditional limits and smug piety. Let us look at these four possibilities more closely.

The disorder of contemporary life is indisputable. Its violence, both criminal and international, has all but bewildered us. Its disorders, particularly in adolescent years, are frightening. The rebellion against current mores creates wild, neurotic aberrations in the frantic hope of a better sanity. The tranquilizers, the narcotics, the flight from authority and responsibility, the collective neuroses, the paradox of Zen and rumbles, riots and wreckage, all point to an essential disorder at the human level.

At the center of such disorder the church stands without any clear counsel. Its own affairs are measured by the moral criteria of industry in terms of quantity, success, and prestige. While its own motives are thus generated, its voice is raised either in the vague terms of being good, or of conforming to middle-class respectability, or of eschewing the pioneer pleasures of "wine, women, and song." There are literally so many different systems of moral order now wrapped up in the life of the church, it is little wonder that there is widespread confusion. Shall we be good according to the Beatitudes or according to the Greek ideal? According to the Old Testament or medieval notions? According to the Renaissance or the Industrial Revolution? According to Moses or Rousseau or Freud?

What is needed is the delineation of an order of human life, sufficiently discriminating to possess its own discipline, but attractive enough to promise man more freedom, more sanity, more lasting satisfaction than he is now discovering in his bewildered, haunted, frantically driven, anxiety-ridden existence. He has essentially lost control of his own life, and finds it at the mercy of a dozen devils, each with his own justifications. Religion must find a way to establish a *style,* a distinct way to live, not easily confused with other ways. The early Christians did it, the Franciscans did it, the Puritans did it. We ought to do it, first because we ourselves need to, and secondly, because the world hungers for it.

One thing must be said. It must be an order which respects

a new level of freedom and sophistication achieved by modern man. It cannot be an oversimplified order of Nay-saying. We have had too much of that in Protestanism, and equally in Catholicism, from which Protestantism inherited more than it was willing to acknowledge. The natural life and the re-deemed life are not diametrically opposed, any more than creation is denied by redemption. We need to say Yea more emphatically, more reverently, more thankfully, to the simple realities and experiences of human life. Our humanity—imper-fect as it is—needs to be confirmed religiously. This is the beginning of a Christian moral order—namely, that man as man takes priority over thing and idea and tradition.

In the second place, religion must reach a new depth of mystery. This will mean a number of things. It will curtail a lot of pompous pretension of ecclesiastical conceit. It will un-dercut much traditional dogmatism, fanaticism, and overwean-ing nonsense about being in possession of special revelations. It will introduce a new sense of modesty, a fresh and real humility, an antiseptic honesty in the face of life's terror, its inexplicable anguish, and its profound contradictions. It will wipe the whitewash off the grim-jawed face of Job and look squarely in the eyes of one who said, "My God, my God, why hast Thou forsaken me!" It will mean moving beyond the safe superficiality of those satiated by facts and information or those busy as hell's demons organizing the dry husks of a grainless harvest! It means recovering a new vision of excellence in the savor of life's events, a new reflectiveness, a new patience to stand and wait before the humblest occasion until it gives up its secret. It means a new willingness to look like a fool, prob-ing at some unimportant point in time or place, while the crowds follow the big noise, the long parade, the crowned monarch.

All these things I have said because they are only preamble

for saying what I find very hard to say, very hard because it is too easy to say. The new depth of mystery which religion must penetrate in our day to be vital is God Himself. He is the essential mystery, not a debatable idea. He is the strange and forbidding depth to the floating sophistication on the surface of our educated world. He is the denial of the old idolatries which we thought forever dead, and which we see again renewed in our comfortable churches and tight little orthodoxies. Wherever life and death meet face to face in their ineluctable struggle, where evil strips itself of every excuse, and where goodness dares to be utterly gratuitous, beyond all shrewdness and caution, under every fact and fiction, at the still center of the turning wheel of time, there the mystery stands and the bush in the wilderness burns and yet turns not to ash. The recovery of a greater depth in religion is the accomplishment of a new modesty, an excitement born of talking about God in a new way.

If we can achieve these two things, namely, a new style of human life lived in a new depth of mystery, we may be able to go on to the third possibility of change, which is to indulge ourselves in a fresh thrust of the imagination, in striking syntheses, bold images, and vital liturgies by which the human spirit may play the flickering shadows of its faith against the dark inscrutable terrors of this life. We need to celebrate with fresh spontaneity and recklessness the fire of our freedom, the agony of our joys, the cry and caring of the cross, the stubborn hammering of our hunger on the gates of high heaven, the benedictions of our flesh and the epiphanies of the hidden God. We need to sing and shout in new creations, careless of our reputation, carried beyond custom and cliché, beyond the ruts of routine, until the new creation is revealed. The scandal of our worship is its fastidious boredom.

By thus learning to worship, by offering the world religion's best gift, namely, the way to remember and re-enact with thanksgiving the astonishing presence of God in the world, we may at the same time come into the fourth possibility of faith, a new dimension of compassion. If the liturgy has become a way we conform to safety, then compassion has been transferred to the collective church and calcified in organized agencies. Albert Camus' brilliant and justified attack on the safe but hypocritical compassion of the Christian church during the war years is well known. We have institutionalized compassion while our own imagination in the ways of human caring was atrophied. We sent hired agents to do at the ends of the world what we refused to do at our own front doors. We romanticized our caring at long distance, and became hard and ruthless in our social blindness at home. The judgment day is hard upon us; the mock benevolence of delegated compassion no longer shields us; the scrimpy limits of good will no longer cover the naked reality of our hidden hate and nasty prejudice. Unless we find some way to enlarge our hearts, our Christian faith will stand ashamed before the dimensions of political concern and international care. Until we move beyond the snug limits of our middle-class conceits, our faith will be too small to handle the binding of this society together in any bonds of peace. Indeed, we may have to turn our back on the church with a solemn disregard for its respectability and prestige before we can act like Christians in the face of this world's need.

These four things we need: a new moral order, more distinctive, more discriminating, with greater room for freedom and sophistication; a greater sense of mortal mystery, a fresh sense of modesty, to abjure the old conceits and idolatries; a boldness and spontaneity to express ourselves vigorously and joyously in the act of worship; and a larger compassion, less stultified by class vanity and church pride.

To paraphrase Christopher Fry: The frozen misery of centuries breaks, cracks, begins to move—there is thunder in the floes . . . the thaw, the flood, the upstart Spring . . . Thank God our time is now—we take the longest stride men ever took. . .

THE ECUMENICAL
CROSS

An American businessman, Clarence Randall, one-time president of the Inland Steel Company, writing in *The Atlantic Monthly* for May 1963, describes "Table Mountain at the southern tip of South Africa, flanked on the right by Lion's Head and on the left by Devil's Head, [as it] looks down on the rock point which divides the Indian and Atlantic Oceans. When the first white man saw this dramatic headland rising from the open sea, he named it the Cape of Storms. Many years later some canny Dutch burgher renamed it the Cape of Good Hope, and today the whole world waits anxiously to know which man was right."

If I may extrapolate from geography to history, from space to time, a similar declaration might be made of our century. As we moved into the twentieth, the time became a veritable Cape of Storms, violent beyond description. Not only empires were wrecked, but vast orders of habit and belief were demolished, old certainties and traditional ideals were lost, and mankind faced a new depth of despair and doubt. Yet along with the terror and hopelessness, with the war and mortal anguish, immense struggle took place to wrest from the very "storms of destruction" a new and more lasting victory for hope. Our age, unprecedented in violence and horror, is equally unprecedented in compassion and concern. We have moved into a larger world, undoubtedly accompanied by greater risks, but at the same time with the promise of larger benedictions. All of us wait with eager and uneasy hearts to see whether the Cape of Storms may not be the Cape of Good Hope.

When the world moves into a new age, religion has a job

Given at Weston College, Weston, Massachusetts, and published in *Thought* (Fordham University Quarterly), vol. 40 (Spring 1965).

to do. If the foundations have been shaken, as they have been in our time, faith will need a steady hand and a clear eye to make the right decisions and to guide men lest they be confused by their own frenzy or destroyed by folly. If the old landmarks have disappeared and the customs and traditions of the past forgotten or obscured by new ways, then reverence must sharpen its sight and look to its loyalties, lest it give itself to spurious ghosts or aggressive novelties.

There will be anxieties and fears and deep distresses of the spirit; there will be a vain nostalgia of glories long gone and a struggle to keep hope alive; there will be darkness and agony of soul, and many, many Gethsemanes. We shall find our strength tested, our prayers bewildered, our motives questioned, our wisdom suspect—and, most of all, our mission and message will meet with scrutiny and penetrating criticism. Whenever the shape of the world by which men live changes, with the changing of the guard when a King Uzziah dies, religion must labor to keep her balance and prove her integrity.

This moment is such a time. The true nature of modernity, scarcely suspected at the turn of the century, is being disclosed in a series of breathtaking glimpses of a new world. The work of the last three or four centuries is being unveiled with a ruthless and devastating thoroughness. The horrors of war possible in a technical civilization are literally beyond imagination. The transformation of society into megalopolis, the obsessive fury induced by industry into human activity, the changed mores and attitudes of the masses, all point to an apocalyptic hour in which faith, if it is to be at all effective, must find a way to face the time and speak the language of our fellows.

Professor Amos Wilder, in his deeply discerning book, *The Language of the Gospel*,[1] refers to W. MacNeile Dixon's statement in the Gifford Lectures on "The Human Situation."

---

[1] New York: Harper and Row, 1964.

Nature . . . is implacable and restless and countenances no calm, no stagnation throughout her vast estate. If we are to understand matters aright *we must think in terms of convulsions* . . . To get the scale of cosmic things we must perceive nature for what she is, as everlastingly and furiously dynamic. . . . Life is a perilous adventure (p. 60).

Surely nothing in the contemporary events has been more dramatic in its inception or more significant in its consequences than the arrival of the ecumenical age. When the late Pope John XXIII announced his intention of convening an ecumenical council, few dreamed of, or subsequently doubted, the profound conviction out of which the decision came or foresaw the changes which would ensue. That it changed the religious climate of the world, no one can deny. That it did so with such rejoicing indicates how much Christendom desired it. The log jam of centuries, the tangled bitterness and envy, the paralysis of separateness and hostility, the inertia of prejudice and ignorance, the insidious pride and controversial defensiveness were suddenly relaxed. To be sure, they were not all swept away, but the imponderable victory of a new climate manifested itself firmly and tenaciously. A new age was born —the ecumenical age—born in a world ashamed of its Dachaus and Hiroshimas, frightened of its political paranoia, dismayed with its disintegrating order, and sick with disbelief. One man, perhaps the one least expected to generate such a climate, did with simplicity and humbleness of heart what statesmen and erudite theologians had failed to do. Startling as the statement seems, Pope John, by the warmth of his spirit and the lack of formal posture, redeemed the world—and particularly us Christians, who scarcely believed it could be done. After all, history is stubborn, institutions are rigid, and people are cynical and sinful. But the gospel is still true, that the poor in spirit or the pure in spirit may accomplish what the powerful or the erudite may fail to do.

Yet what Pope John accomplished is not the end of the matter. He opened the door; whether or not we are willing to enter the ecumenical age wholeheartedly still remains for us to decide. We have scarcely begun to measure the opportunities which are unfolding before our sight. And far more awaits us if we have courage and passion to continue. The new dimensions of fellowship we have begun to taste, and the larger vistas of truth which may become ours excite us with a joy like that of discovering a new land.

On the other hand, we must be aware that the changes that have been wrought by the ecumenical spirit do not usher us into any kind of Utopia, secular or sacred, Christian or otherwise. The ecumenical age will double our opportunities in many directions, but it will also double our responsibilities. It will deepen our joys, but it will increase our dangers. It will liberate us from many false prejudices, but it will lure us also by numerous false hopes. It will broaden our trust and extend our compassion, but it will also demand a higher faith and a keener sense of human need. In short, the ecumenical spirit will have painful responsibilities as well as pleasurable satisfactions. As Christians we need to be realistic lest we assume too easily that the victory is already ours, when in truth the trumpet call has just been sounded.

It is for such reasons that we must face the reality of what can only be called "the ecumenical cross." If we are faithful to the possibilities which we see in this new age, we shall know sacrifice and suffering. The extraordinary good will which Pope John generated will not be sufficient to carry us willy-nilly into the Promised Land. There is a wilderness to traverse, there are temptations to confront, problems to solve, and a deeper level of spiritual obedience to be attained before we can claim what may seem at times to be inevitable. The cross is not imposed; it is implicit in the situation.

As the writer of Proverbs was wont to say in olden times, there are three things, yea, a fourth. I should like to transfer the simple mannerism to matters which must concern us as serious Christian responsibilities in the ecumenical age: three things and a fourth, and the fourth is the most difficult cross of all. Unless we bear that one well, the other three will scarcely be more than gestures of a thoughtless hand.

What are the three? The first is that we must recover the glad news of God's activity in the world in such a way as to provide all Christians with an exuberant joy and an ineffable peace. We are not doing so at present. The wineskins of the ancient gospel have hardened, the forms in which the gaiety of faith was first communicated have become dull and rigid. The shout of great rejoicing and spontaneity has turned to the yawn of boredom. Everywhere, in every church, there are more people than one would wish trying to wring out of the dry and sterile habits of the past a drop of simple glory, a sign of refreshing mercy. We who were to keep the spring clear so the waters of God might run down like rivers have cluttered and complicated the sweet grace of the living God with our clever plumbing and our ecclesiastical proprieties.

Put it another way: We must uncover a deeper level of the gospel if we are not only to sustain the freshness and vigor of our faith but also to provide that larger dimension of God's mystery and glory in which our historical differences assume their proper place, and perchance, God willing, be transcended in a revelation larger than either of our traditions. Technical adjustments in ecclesiastical relations will not help us. Nor will the most tactful of suave diplomacies and the most affable of official courtesies. Only a new depth of grace to stand the long, long pull of the ropes binding the old adversaries together will do. Only a mystery of God deep enough to humble us beyond our present pride of position, beyond our traditional defenses, beyond our self-assured righteousness, will do. This new breadth of vision, this new hospitality of heart, this new and breath-taking *koinonia,* will only be firm if we can enlarge and strengthen the foundations. We must go deeper into our humanity—that is costly. But there is no other way to strengthen the stakes when the tent is spread so wide.

There is a second cross to be borne if we are to be responsible as Christians in this ecumenical age. Out of this new depth of the gospel we must learn to speak to a world radically displaced from the cultural traditions of the past, both biblical and classical. A new way of life has been initiated, born of a series of revolutions, both social and intellectual, from which men have derived a new set of mores as well as new illusions and new fears. For a long time we have either rejected the revolutions out of hand or neglected to estimate their character and meaning. We are woefully behind on our homework. Freud and Marx, science and industry, automation and urbanization, atomic energy and space travel stand peering in the windows of our sanctuaries while we act as if they are not there.

It is the first duty of religion to evaluate the meaning of historical happenings. This is the essence of prophecy. To speak with bolder insight and to judge with more discrimination in the confusion of the present hour is a prime necessity. Better to make a mistake than to hide in safety.

The world, if we can speak so generally, is carrying enormous burdens. Destiny has its enigmatic face up against ours. We live in daily anxiety. The nations are nervous, wary; the people are uneasy, suspicious. All kinds of men in all kinds of responsible positions are tangled in the knot of history and bear their pain manfully. When will we understand their agony, their torment of conscience, their hunger for light, their suffering to decide? When will we respect their labor in the dark obscurities of the present? When will we speak perceptively of the accomplishments of politician, artist, industrialist, scientist? We must find the glad news again, not only in the sacred pages of our ancient texts but also immediately in the lives of men hard-pushed by the exigencies of the times, in the unsuspected Gethsemanes of secular agony.

This brings me to the third point where we must face our responsibility if we are to enter into the works of faith by which the ecumenical age may realize itself. We must find new resources of compassion. As Christians, our faces have been red with shame ever since Albert Camus administered his well-deserved rebuke of what I can only call our collectivized compassion. For multitudes, compassion is safely vested in the corporate structure of the church, to be handled by the usual machinery of clergy and missionaries. How many anomalies this produces, I need not enumerate. The limits of benevolence run too close to the restrictions of respectability and prudence to be more than a scrimped and cautious device manipulated for the sake of a comfortable conscience rather than the redemptive reflection of Christ's breathtaking love and God's everlasting mercy.

We must begin to see that compassion, the willingness to suffer for others, the selflessness we have associated with sainthood, have actually caught on in the world so that the profound awareness of men's needs and the passionate desire to be of help are now part of the social pattern and quite often self-consciously separated from any religious ground. In the characteristically endless conferences to which we in America are addicted, I am amazed time and time again to see the depth of human concern, the earnestness of reform, the liveliness of conscience among government leaders, journalists, industrialists, and politicians. Just as in the race problem, where the church tends to be the last and most stubborn bastion of segregation, so in many social fields our conscience seems strapped and shackled to nineteenth-century ideas of respectability rather than twentieth-century practical righteousness. It will be easy to lag so far behind in matters of social compassion that the world may come to believe we are interested in our institutional success rather than the succor of men.

These, then, are three of the costly responsibilities of the ecumenical age into which Pope John so magnificently and so modestly introduced us, and which Pope Paul now labors to advance and maintain. We shall need to penetrate to a new level of the gospel to sustain the heavy strain of bringing together in meaningful relationship the two estranged traditions of our faith. Moreover, we shall have to find the insight and imagination to bridge the gulf between the church and the world and to find a language in which the world's experience and our ancient heritage are equally acknowledged. And our compassion must be reborn, refreshed, revitalized, both in quality and dimension, to match the vast and imponderable agony of the modern world.

But I said that besides these three there is a fourth responsibility, the heaviest of them all. It is not complicated or abstruse, hard to understand or difficult to imagine. It is ourselves. In a sense this is our hardest cross, our deepest embarrassment, our most aggravating frustration. If the ecumenical gambit fails, it will not be for want of councils, theologians, high ideals, or noble purposes—it will be because you and I will have failed to match the greatness of our day with souls of such stature that the new dream will flow through our deeds and be fashioned in our action.

There is no way to recover the freshness and power of the gospel sufficiently to bind all Christians together in a passionate, if perchance at times uncomfortable, unity without pushing our hearts and minds to heights and depths far beyond the easy limits we have already attained. We will never speak to this world as long as we rest content with the words which our fathers spoke and make no effort to hammer out on the anvil of our own hearts the new words for reaching the transcendent realities of faith. There is no way to share in the agony of our world, its darkness and shame and bewilderment, except by suffering what it suffers, carrying in our hearts what it carries in its heart, and sweating through the Gethsemane of its travail and decision.

The shame of it all is simply that we can get by with less. We can have Christianity enough to satisfy the minimum demands—to be respectable, to be revered, even to be popular, without having enough to match the magnitude of need in an ecumenical age. To recover the freshness until our faith sings and dances in delight; to walk into God's world, expecting to find him and able to point him out to busy men; to plunge into humanity, to take our place with it, to laugh and cry, to be ashamed and forgiven and believed, to suffer and rejoice with it—this is both the measure of our loyalty to Christ and our faithfulness to the ecumenical age.

THE MYSTERY OF
OUR CALLING

W hat kind of hearts do we have, that they are not satisfied to take things as they are, this great obvious world, this rushing stream of life? What is it that flickers at the edge of all plain facts and shines through solid circumstances, and calls our souls from the flesh to feed on the subtle substance of a glory few men see? Why do we push beyond dollars and cents, routine and repute, and dabble in beauty and stretch our minds for truth? Why are we tormented by this kind of freedom, haunted by something beyond us, tempted and teased out of all comfort by ghosts which come and go, and leave us like pilgrims on a long, long road where the inns are few and far between?

Embedded somewhere in the darkness of a fantasy I can never forget, there is a scene in which the mystery of our calling is conjured up most dramatically. It is the empty carpenter shop from which Jesus walked to go down to the Jordan to begin his ministry. There is no text or scripture but I can easily see Jesus working there, making ox yokes and door lintels, hefting the wood, fitting the tenons and mortises, sawing, planing, stacking the boards. I can see him eyeing his customers, fitting into the village life, dependable, competent. Why did he shut up shop, lay down his tools, brush off the shavings from his work clothes, clear the bench and walk out into the world? Why did he quit doing what his neighbors could understand, turn his back on his reputation and start on a new path, doing things they could not understand? When did he first see something in the wood, beyond the shavings

Given at Harvard Divinity School and published in its *Bulletin*, October 1961.

that curled from his plane? When did he stand still, seeing what no man could see, and hearing what no ear could hear? When did the call come?

His followers were never sure. Some thought he didn't hear it until the baptism at the Jordan. Others were sure he knew it earlier, when he was twelve, and stayed with the doctors in the temple. Still others thought his call was coincident with his birth, signalized by a star, and others that it was the intention of God before the world began. We simply do not know. Perhaps it came in a thousand ways, infinitely pouring in from the Father's love and glory through all the tiny chinks of life and the world.

The same mystery is in his disciples. They had jobs, homes, families. They gathered taxes, fished in the sea, sold at market, held jobs in business—and then they startled everyone. They walked away from their desks, dropped their nets, even abandoned their families. They were never quite the same. What had happened? What mystery had opened their hearts and spilled them into history?

You and I have been touched by this flame, elusively, hauntingly, irrevocably. We have been thrust into an ineluctable hunger for something beyond self or earth, beyond peace or even love. We have been thrust out, pushed forward. We are ill at ease with the obvious. We are caught between what people understand and what none of us understand. We may seem like fools, especially to the prudent and worldly wise, and often to ourselves we confess we are fools. We stand fumbling at the latch of life, elated and disturbed, hoping and fearing, certain and unsure at the same time. When were we called? And how? Have we shut up shop, or do we still keep the key so we can slip back and start business again? How firm is our face set out toward the unknown tomorrow?

No wonder the shifting, changing opinions in Jeremiah's day, thrown up by the chaos of life and catastrophe, gave rise to the great poignant hope of a new covenant, a new call, absolutely certain, unmistakable, written in the very fibers of the heart, undoubted and unconfused. How good it would be if our call, the covenent of our tie with God, could be so far beyond cavil, so unmistakably at the core of self, so near the center that we could not question it.

Or again, if we turn to the magnificent vision of Paul in Romans where he calls up the anguish and travail of all creation, we can see the vast drama of man's slow and painful climb to reach at last the climax where all things come clear in the manifestation of the sons of God, men whose faith and vision would hold in one great order of joy and peace the age-old contradictions and terrors of the world. Here the call comes to a focus; the sons of God, men whom he calls, now bring creation to fulfillment. A great vision, grandly conceived and boldly proclaimed!

Well, let's be honest. The image of our calling is not as certain as though it were written into our being or as powerfully compelling as the vision of Paul. The truth is that it has been rudely assaulted, rubbed out, obscured, and generally confused. Both in the ministry itself and in church members in general, we are not sure what the calling is. Men are asking why be ordained, or if we are to be ordained, how can we make it something more than a formality, bereft of either *mysterium tremendum* or *mysterium fascinans?* Indeed we wonder if the minister isn't really a man without a job, no longer in possession of any real function in a technological society. If originally there was a great mystery in our calling, now it seems as if we have been called to something of a mystery.

The astonishing thing about this situation is that precisely at the moment when the church is no longer certain of what our calling means, contemporary literature and the arts have rediscovered the heroic dimensions of the essentially religious man. Compounded of the features drawn directly from the New Testament or the lives of the saints, these writers are celebrating the manifestation of the sons of God as if the new law were written indelibly in their very flesh. There is no uncertainty here, no vague dabbling, no cloudy mysticism, no vapid sentimentality. While the religious man has lost definition and clarity in the ministry and the church, novels, poems, and paintings have reasserted the shape and sign of the new saint in a new age.

Time would fail me to tell of all of them. There is Murica in Silone's *Bread and Wine,* Rieux in Camus' *The Plague,* Faulkner's Dilsey in *The Sound and Fury,* Bernanos' stupid priest in *Diary of a Country Priest,* Greene's drunken priest in *The Power and the Glory,* the tramps of Beckett and the old man of Hemingway. The list could be extended in all directions.

The testimony is plain. There is a calling, a great and high calling, open to risks and profound danger, to be bought at a price, to be denied at the cost of a betrayed destiny. We may have difficulty seeing it in a clear concise outline, but the reason, I suspect, is that we are cautious and hold ourselves from it. I confess I have my own confusions, but I have seen it in part, and it is only in part because I have partly given myself and partly withheld myself. I have come near it in those who have answered fully. And this is what I have seen.

In the first place, to be called is not to be called away from our humanity, but back into it. We are forever trying to escape the exigencies of our mortal condition, and the call from God is taken too often to mean a surcease of suffering the burden of being human. We become detached from mankind, assume a semidivine posture of being above the common embarrassment of doubt and shame, and begin to mouth the phrases of faith wrung from men who laid hold on heaven while they suffered the torture of hell.

One is reminded of Captain McWhirr in Conrad's *Typhoon:*

Captain McWhirr had sailed over the surface of the oceans as some men go skimming over the years of existence to sink gently into a placid grave, ignorant of life to the last, without ever having been made to see all it may contain of perfidy, of violence, and of terror. There are on sea and land such men thus fortunate—or thus disdained—by destiny or by the sea.

The witness alike of Jesus, or the prophets, or the saints is that once God's call comes we are plunged headlong into the sufferings of mankind. For the first time we are on the inside of this world's pain, no longer separated from any man's anguish or sin. This is Dostoevski's plea in the monk Zossima's great testimony in *Brothers Karamazov:*

If the evil-doing of men moves you to indignation and overwhelming distress, even to a desire for vengeance on the evildoers, shun above all things that feeling. Go at once and seek suffering for yourself, as though you were yourself guilty of that wrong. Accept that suffering and bear it and your heart will find comfort, and you will understand that you too are guilty, for you might have been a light to the evil-doers, even as the one man sinless, and you were not a light to them.

Among our modern authors this call to share in the suffering of men is illuminated and profoundly stressed by André Malraux and Albert Camus, neither of them Christian in the normal sense of that term. Malraux boldly speaks of the "joy of fraternal pain" and believes no man becomes himself until he shares the deepest level of unity with his death-threatened and bludgeoned fellow men. Camus' voice, now silenced, was never more impassioned than when he asked men to rise to a new level of compassion. His rebuke of the Dominicans in which he included all Christians was to call into question their fake concern, uttered in credo and prayer, but conveniently limited in practice to comfortable condescensions.

No, the truth of it is that in God's call we are called back, so to speak, called back from our pretensions, our poses, our holy false faces, back and down and into the very conditions we sought to escape, that we might be tremblingly alive where honest people live, and where if God has any concern at all for them, he will be found.

This last phrase brings me to the second marked point of clarity in the call as testified to by Jesus' ministry and the work of men of God, namely, that they are all called to "salvage the remains of sanctity" in men's blundering hearts. None of us lives long without bringing down about our heads a great clutter of rubbish. We lose ourselves in it. We sometimes try to shape it up as if it would carry the weight of truth or beauty and withstand the storms of tragic reality. It is a pathetic business until someone with eyes to see, and the gentlest as well as the severest kind of perceptiveness, walks in and points out where the real blessing of God rests, where there is something sacred in which our hearts can find peace and joy forever. This is our call to rightly divide the Word—ah, you thought surely I was about to say the "Word of Truth" as if it meant the texts of the Holy Scripture, but I must say that is but part of the matter and tends often to be merely technical. No, it is our calling to rightly divide the Word—in the human heart—from the words which are there in great clamoring throngs—and that is not an easy thing.

Indeed, it is a rather sad fact that in our day there is much disillusionment about sanctity. The term has been corrupted by the church itself. It has become formalized, falsified, encrusted with jewels and crawling with spurious pictures. Protestantism is not without its share of responsibility in neutralizing the life of the world. For many, the holy seems a bit like superstition, once it is taken out of the realm of generalities and applied to anything specific.

Yet, if we cannot find sanctity, we should be honest and give over the game to those who say God is dead, for sanctity is the moment of his presence; we should give up worship, which seeks to remember and to re-enact the primordial events of sanctity through which God manifested his place in the world; we should give up any moral seriousness, for without sanctity, morality becomes a convenient pattern of mores and nothing more.

It is a significant thing that it is this, precisely this sense of sanctity, which breaks through the prose of Hemingway, or the squalor of Graham Greene's stories, or the tortured complexities of decadence in Faulkner's novels. In the latter's *As I lay Dying*, through all the stupidity, ordinary human shamefulness, and downright messiness, there runs the thin thread of Anse's promise to Addie that he would bury her with her folks in Jefferson, and in spite of a veritable Odyssey of troubles, he stubbornly refuses to abate his pledge. In the midst of weakness, humor, natural catastrophes, nevertheless the sanctity of the promise is kept. Perhaps this is mankind's last claim on the title of being human. This is our call, to find in man's much-beleaguered heart, fraught with every shame and embarrassment, living on the brink of endless decisions in which heaven and hell are always bidding for his soul, here amid the ruins of his dreams and the cheap rubbish he is forever gathering to his heart, we must find the scraps and vestiges of the divine presence, hidden, obscured, and often lost.

And this leads now to the third unmistakable mark of the calling. Louis Lavelle describes it in his *Meaning of Holiness*[1] when he says of the saint that "through his presence alone he succeeds in giving to the things or persons he meets on the way the *interior quality they lacked.*" The severest desolation is the emptying out of life, the sickening sense of the abyss, the awful taste of nothingness. And in this wild and furious world of machines and techniques, of manipulation and screaming salesmen, men and women are externalized, whirled about until there is no inner life left in them. They become masks, routines, functions, reputations, successes, without any specific gravity. We see ourselves in the terrible shapes of Richier and Paolozzi, or in the disgusting and haunted degradations of Dubuffet and Oliveira.

Our calling is to restore an interior quality to life, to supply what has been lacking in the realm of inanimate nature, and to assist our fellow men by sustaining the inwardness of the spirit. In short, our job is to rehabilitate people inwardly, to engage in such a relationship that they may become themselves as persons, to encourage by our anticipation and imagination the exercise of their souls. It is one of the sacramental powers of the spirit of man, once liberated by the call, to give men meaning, to touch them to life, to restore their souls.

However mysterious our call may be, it is embedded deeply in the very mystery by which we are human beings. There is no way for us to detour or avoid the inevitability of doing something with things as they are; only one thing we cannot

[1] New York: Pantheon, 1954.

do—we cannot leave them as they are. Man extends so far into the world that it cannot be totally extricated from him, and the world is so much part of man's substance that he cannot be known as if he existed by himself. We change whatever it is "out there" by the alchemy of our own freedom. By being human, we stand at the center of creation, where things are changed and the world is lifted or debased by the twist of our desire.

A CHARACTER IN
SEARCH OF A ROLE

Some years ago, Luigi Pirandello, one of Italy's great playwrights, wrote a very provocative play called *Six Characters in Search of an Author*. The whole world, as Shakespeare pointed out, is a stage, and we strut across it to play our brief part, with words and gestures that fit, we hope, the total situation and make sense both to the other actors and to the audience.

But if one of the actors does not know his role, if he comes on dressed as a king and there is no part for a king and no serfs or subjects to acknowledge him as king, and if everyone else on stage is dressed in sport shirts or Roman togas, then he appears out of place, irrelevant, somewhat ridiculous. If he begins to talk Elizabethan rhetoric in the midst of East Harlem slang or beatnik jargon, the play falls apart. There has to be some common ground of discourse to hold things together or else the action is stalemated. If, for instance, in the midst of a scene laid in a Victorian parlor full of bric-a-brac, with people in the incredibly fussy fashion of wasp-waisted ladies and frock-coated gentlemen, a character dressed like Amenhotep the Third stalked in, it would not take long to decide that he was an anachronism, that he did not belong there, and that he must have been badly muddled to have come on stage at all.

There is one character in the modern world who is deeply bewildered about his place on the stage of the twentieth century. In many scenes he seems to be utterly out of place, an anachronism, if ever there was one. I speak of the minister, the priest, the man of God. What is his cue for entering the

Given at St. Paul School of Theology (Methodist), published in *The Journal*, Spring 1965.

play? When should he appear, and when should he leave? What is his proper garb, his appropriate gesture, the sign of his calling? Should he wear vestments, or a bow tie, or a Prince Albert? Should he kneel, or fold his hands, or slap everybody on the back as if he knew them? Should he freeze his face in a perpetual pious smirk, or should he have a crew cut and swear a little? Should he stay with the ladies for missionary chatter, or hobnob in the smoker where politics and taxes are the order of the day? Is he just the man for funerals, marriages, and christenings, but otherwise as much wanted as a sore thumb?

The question is not as frivolous as it seems. The question at the bottom is how religion fits into a technological world and culture; how churches take their place in twentieth-century society. How do ministers really converse with the other actors on the stage today? In Pirandello's play, *Six Characters in Search of an Author,* a group of actors are already rehearsing when the curtain rises on the first act. Quite abruptly they are interrupted by the arrival of a family—a man and his wife, their grown son and grown daughter, and two small children. These people immediately push into the play and want to take part in it. The actors resist. After all, they do not want their lines twisted askew or their neatly laid plans complicated by outsiders. Perhaps it is not too wide of the mark to suggest that we who are in the "establishment" are often much more concerned to keep the traditional play going with all its carefully rehearsed lines and gestures than to admit the realities of living characters who blunder in with all sorts of difficulties, mysteries, and even scandals. We in the church want people all right; no doubt of that. But we want them to learn our lines, to use our gestures, to dress in our style, to play our play—in short, we call the tune, and if they conform, we are sure they will be saved. In Pirandello's play, it does not work out that way. By the end of the play, the characters, unruly as they are, become real and grip our imagination and sympathy, while the actors dwindle and fade in spite of their fine posturings and well-trimmed lines.

What role shall the minister play? He has been called of God and, whatever he does, he should play it manfully and to the hilt, with as much intelligence and force as he can muster. The play is already in progress, and others have made their entrance, not by our pleasure but by the will of Him who sent them. That the minister will be resisted by some of the actors already on the stage should not surprise us. We cannot write a new script or insist on our selection of the cast, except in the dubious manner of ecclesiastical snobbery which refuses to talk with anyone who is not our kind of Christian. We have been flung into the action, into the very middle of things, and we must decide what stance to take, what words to say, what action to portray. We can talk with the world, or we can trump up some kind of make-believe, as pretentious as Solomon, out of the past, or out of our dreams, or out of our pride. But play we must, until the final act comes and death leads us off into the wings.

The puzzle is not an easy one to solve. How do we talk to a world about meekness and humility when it moves and lives and has all its inner drives in ambition and success? How shall we talk about the cross and suffering when its great passion is for comfort and the elimination of the smallest inconveniences? How do we make any sense out of the need for redemption when most people would rather be well-insured than saved? How does one speak intelligibly about compassion when the church cares more for its reputation than for people? How can we converse about being poor in order to achieve integrity and simplicity when our whole society wants nothing more than to be prosperous, a willing slave to bigger and better status symbols? What is our role in a world where the connection with the primordial revelations of the Bible has been lost? What is our role in a society conditioned by the scientific criterion of truth, motivated by the industrial mores of ambition and prestige, and enamored by its faith in the omnipotence of techniques to reach any goal without changing the nature of man?

Let us make a beginning. One might assume that the first and most unmistakable element in the role of the minister is in his care of the church. The rub comes, however, when we ask what we mean by the care of the church. If we mean merely that it is our job to maintain the institution at any cost, to make it bigger and richer, more popular and better organized, then I begin to balk. To care for the church is to bring it back to itself, to keep alive in it those ancient splendors of the spirit, to nurture its quiet dependence on God, to return it to repentance and modesty, to purge it of arrogance and stupidity, to deepen its compassion, to puncture its vanity, to breach its petty limits, to encourage its honesty, and to confirm it when it is authentic. To care for the church may mean having a sharper discrimination and a more penetrating insight about what makes a church responsive to the living pressure of God, or what transforms it until it is no more than a desperate means to avoid God's judgment, an escape from our true humanity, a buffer between ourselves and reality. Indeed, the care of the church may mean making it smaller, even poorer, and perhaps running the risk of its being thought a failure in order to make it a house of prayer where all men may see in the mystery of their lives the wonder of the Everlasting God.

There is no doubt that the minister has a role in this chrome-plated, gadget-crazy, haste-driven culture, if he will see to it that the church provides people with an environment where they can recover the essential mystery of their lives and confirm their identity. The church has no business obscuring their doubts and fears, or ignoring their confusion and embarrassment. It should not blot out their inner lives by an incessant storm of spurious ecclesiastical activities. It should not smother the sight of God's intimate working with their souls by addicting them to the standard brands of piety. It should not feed them easy tranquilizers of cheap grace or positive thinking when God himself is trying to upset their self-complacency.

In a world like ours where our humanity is forever being lost in vast mechanistic complexes, where we take on the attributes of machines, where the feeling of being human is under the grinding wear and tear of attrition, the church can save souls only to the extent it can keep people human in every dimension of that term. That means helping them to be honest—a very difficult task, especially in a respectable church and in the climate of frenetic optimism characteristic of American culture. It means being open to judgment and aware of one's own everlasting need. It means the reinvigoration of compassion, which we have collectivized in missions so we did not have to be compassionate personally, dispensing our mercy in far-off places and through paid agents. In short, the church ought to redeem people from being *un*people; it ought to redeem them from their religion, their churchiness, their unreality, their pretenses and self-deceptions. Nothing worse can be said of the church than that it is awfully hard to stay in it and remain real. And the fact is, as soon as people cease to be real, they lose their souls. To care for the church is to love the souls of men more than success.

Now if it be true that this is the basic role of the minister on the stage of this world, then certain other aspects of his distinctive place in our time begin to appear. The first of these is the minister's specific responsibility *to articulate the meaning of human experience.* This may indeed be nothing more than another way of saying save their souls, but saving souls has become so stereotyped that it represents little or nothing real in the present human predicament. Multitudes of people are hungry to know what to make of their lives and come to church hopefully and expectantly to get some help, only to discover that we have our lines down pat, we have learned them well, and we are not going to have them interrupted or questioned. They are the regular stock-in-hand of the church and minister, and we hand it out with unctuous self-satisfaction, although it fits into practically nothing that the individual is suffering or his confusion and torment. It merely adds another layer of smooth, unintelligible patter to a situation already badly garbled. Indeed, we are caught much as the old priest of Graham Greene's play, *The Living Room,* when he says, "I'd like to help you, but whenever I start to say something, the catechism gets in the way."

Surprise is often expressed that so many people in trouble go to psychiatrists instead of seeking the help of their ministers. The reason is not far to find—the psychiatrist is intent on saving the meaning of what happened to the patient and respects it as the only basis of reality and worth. The minister generally is too quick with his conclusions, his answers are given before the whole story is known, and often he has made up his mind before he knows what has happened. He tends to be committed to stereotypes, to think in orthodox terms about life in general, and to impose a whole complex of socially "proper" ideas and "right" opinions over the top of the offering circumstances. The two layers—namely, God's work in the actual circumstances and our overlay of ecclesiastical veneer —have no inner coherence of relationship to each other.

One thing we seem to forget about our human life—meaning is not given with the experience. It comes later, by reflection. It must be dug out, discovered, discerned. Only when we find the right word for it does it come into the clear. Most of the experiences that come to us we lose by never naming them, by failing to identify the meaning or significance. We are, as Rilke puts it, "wasters of sorrow." Such a work is not to be done by a flood of sloppy talk, or a rampage of wild exhortation, or a neat packaging of nice moralisms. It requires penetration, patience, willingness to listen, mercy to forgive, ability to imagine, intelligence to reflect.

The second aspect of the minister's role on the present-day stage of history is that he must be able to recognize and affirm God's *nonecclesiastical activity*. I do not believe that we can act any longer as if the grace of God can be neatly restricted to the church. By implication, at least, Protestantism has made as sharp and invidious division between sacred and secular, divine and human, eternal and temporal, as anyone else. So much so, in fact, that we have largely hidden from ourselves the enormous gulf which exists between the traditional church and the contemporary world. The church has become in our day as thoroughly monastic, that is to say, outside the living issues of actual existence, as the walled colonies of monks in the Middle Ages.

The truth of the matter historically is that the Reformation, which sought to extend the rule of God into secular life and orders, has been gaining considerable ground in the last half-century and has transformed the nature of many secular institutions. We have seen an astonishing development of social responsibility in politics and industry. We have benefited immeasurably by the scientific advances made in medicine, surgery, and psychiatry. And throughout the world of the arts, both literary and plastic, there has been a widespread, brilliant renaissance of religious interest and intent. Nothing is to be gained by acting blind at such points, or by condescendingly insisting that unless these breakthroughs are explicit articulated in traditional Christian forms, they have no validity for the spirit of man. The world, if you will, has been deeply infected by the Christian faith, and on all sides the fruit of it can be seen in new dimensions of human care and spiritual longing.

It is late enough, and perhaps too late, to confront the task of liberating ourselves from the shortsighted stupidity of a fixed iconoclastic attitude of the last three centuries. The minister must become a man of the world. That is to say, he must recognize and affirm the disclosures of human truth in the work of scientists, artists, sociologists, and industrialists of recent history. We are like the Jews who wanted to limit revelation to Moses; we simply have refused to take anything into our Christian faith which has happened in the last three hundred years. The enlargement of understanding about man and the universe, about society and history, still remain "outside the walls." Ministers have a duty to be performed in absorbing such insights and visions into the larger theology of faiths. Until that is done, ministers have no right to complain that they are treated as anachronisms on the stage of the present epoch.

Finally, the third aspect which begins to clarify itself in the role of the minister who faces this age is that he must *help people to worship God.* And I do not mean what is usually meant by the phrase "going to church." A good deal of going to church has little or nothing to do with the worship of God. I mean by worship to celebrate—in joy—the presence of God's living mystery. I mean the persevering search for wholeness, the yearning for clarity, the steadying power of trust. I mean the communion of being, the compassion of each for all, the sense of the human burden, the burden of being human. I mean the insight which plunges into hidden beauty unexpectedly, the doors which open in heavy walls at a touch, the glory that burns in the waste places of the wilderness. I mean the wisdom of being poor, and hungering and thirsting for something only God can give. I mean opening the doors and windows in all directions till the winds of God blow through and the soul is refreshed.

To teach men to worship is not easy in a world where we are always in a hurry, where we are "distracted from distraction by distraction," where the images of God have lost their strength and hang limp, like Dali watches, where the mystery of existence is too deep to bother us in our haste, where we accumulate rather than contemplate, and where we organize rather than redeem. Our tempo is set by the machine, not by the seasons of the eternal. We are more concerned with the appearance than the substance, more with what people may think than with what we are. We prefer to change the world so we do not have to change ourselves, rather than change ourselves to fit our world.

Without worship, men cease to be their total selves. Their vision retreats, their substance thins out, they lose their balance and their weight. They boast and stumble, brag and fumble. Their freedom loses its sanctity, and the future becomes an abyss. Their church-going, when it fails to rise to the heights and depths of worship, becomes boring and deadly.

Moreover, without true worship, there is nothing to hold the world together—no vastness of vision, no firm ground for the pilgrimage from birth to death, no sustaining bond between man and man, no open sky for his shouts of joy or his song of love. No worship means no society. A secular society is a contradiction in terms. Even a Marxist society produces its rituals, its holy days, and its vision of world order!

In a technological age such as ours, the minister may construe his role in either of two ways: he may disregard the age and its culture, its ethos and way of life. He may turn his back on it and enter the church, intent on keeping it safe from everything outside, keeping the script intact, the lines spoken as written, and no interruptions allowed. That can be done and is done. It should be said, however, that there is a great deal of the world already inside. It got there a long time ago and it is not all gospel! On the other hand, he may try to talk to the other actors on the stage, learn their vocabulary, listen to their lines, and make room for their gestures and actions. It will not be easy and it may force the play in new directions. But perhaps we have been in Egypt long enough and need to start the Exodus into a new Promised Land.

The truth is we have been called to be ministers in an age when the traditional role is in transition. We may find it confusing, sometimes embarrassing, but we are responsible for finding our way around such a world, to take our part in the dialogue, and if the script does not always include us, we will have to find some way to explain why we are on the stage and what we intend to do in God's name. However vague our role may seem to the other actors, however mixed up they are or we are, let us not run out on the play. Complicated as the plot is at this late date in history, there has never been a time when the man of religion faced needs of such a magnitude. We are in on the making of a role; there is a place and action waiting if we can get out of the ancient stereotypes and move into the real issues of history and of living men.

EDUCATION FOR
INSECURITY

Conditioned by the technical climate of our time, all of us have come to respect absolute certainty as the operating ideal of our civilization. Induced by scientific precision, our world has come to regard as one of its highest virtues the ability to achieve firm factual information, reliable techniques, and assured consequences. Everywhere—in science, business, industry, and not least in education—we have trained people to cut the edges sharp, to measure down to a fine hairline, and to put into a formula a guaranteed key for controlling a situation. What we want is colloquially rolled up in the phrase "a sure thing." This has come to be for us and our age the sign of truth, and every profession honors it.

Whether we have overreached ourselves, assuming certainty where it does not really exist, is a serious question. We may be expecting too much certainty in realms where we may have to deal with extreme complexity, or even with irrational realities. Dr. John C. Whitehouse, of Johns Hopkins University, speaking at the 150th anniversary of the Massachusetts General Hospital, drew attention to the necessity in medicine "to tolerate uncertainty with equanimity." He continued,

The educational programs generally experienced by physicians of the past few generations have tended . . . to inculcate an expectation of certainty of knowledge and a phobic aversion for and intolerance of *uncertainty,* and the worst offenders have been teachers of science . . . A less dogmatic clinging to presumed certainties, a greater ability to face uncertainty with equanimity, a more generous and wiser sharing

Given at Berkeley Baptist Divinity School. Inaugural Address for Robert J. Arnott, October 13, 1964.

of leadership—all these interrelated manifestations of a good education—might have done much to humanize medical leadership.

To omit an adequate recognition of the variable human factors, both individual and sociological, is a disservice to truth as well as to professional competence.

What it means to transfer this sense of certainty from science and mechanics to the human realm, or more specifically, to religion, is a critical question. The distortions which have occurred when religion attempted to be scientific, or literally accurate, or predictively guaranteed, are too well known to be elaborated. Formulas of such character in religion are achieved at the expense of God's freedom and of man's elusive mystery.

Although we seem to be thoroughly given over to the virtues of absolute certainty, the striking paradox of the situation is that we are suffering from a massive infection of uncertainty. The more we manipulate nature, the more we plan society, economics, and wars, with cybernetic logistics, the more we seem to be confronted with mounting insecurities at the heart of man himself. The certainty of predictability in the inanimate realm has become fantastic, but in the world where persons determine events, no age has been so shockingly surprised, so rudely shamed, by the erratic and the unexpected. The eruption of wars, the demonic violence of fanatics, the easy compliance with fascism and Nazism, the incredible mass murder by gas ovens, nuclear bombs, and absorption bombing—there is simply no end to the evident failure of certainty as a predictive principle at the human level.

Our world is uneasy at best, violently neurotic at its worst. It is thoroughly unsettled, an age of anxiety, fighting its fears with tranquilizers, scapegoats, and paranoid politics. In spite of social security, unemployment compensation, health services, and all kinds of insurance against every imaginable disaster, people are nervous, restless, and disturbed. They move from job to job, from city to city, from party to party, from church to church, and from marriage to marriage. The entire society is in perpetual motion; a kind of compulsive frenzy allows no one to rest; every class, every party, every business, every art, moves in all directions, fearful of standing still, reacting on all sides in nervous jerks, as though there was nothing left to do but to keep moving, even when the purpose of it has been lost. In such a state the connective tissue is rapidly dissolved, and the effort to maintain the articulate substance of community is far beyond normal.

In back of all this shifting mobility (which makes human society look like a maggot hill), there is the accelerated rapidity of incessant change. Nothing remains the same. Regardless of whether it is good or not, an article must be constantly changed in order to sell. Built-in obsolescence, from cars to clothes, shortens the rhythm of purchase and perish. Professions disappear overnight; complex techniques become useless with the twist of a knob. A professor at the Massachusetts Institute of Technology complains that the instruction he gives will be obsolete by the time the students get a degree for learning it! Everywhere continuity is in shambles, cut and chewed by the incessant chomping of the jaws of progress.

This is the world candidates for the ministry will enter. No wonder they are perplexed as to the role of religion in such a world, or whether their job will be more like that of a museum guard than a creative member of society! No wonder they are bewildered by the sight of the ecclesiastical gigantosaurus refusing to adjust to the conditions of a new climate! No wonder they stand nonplused between a church that does not seem to come alive except for statistics and a world that moves blindly from nightmare to nightmare.

Obviously there was a time—and some of us can remember it quite well—when it seemed legitimate to train ministers as their fathers had been trained, and to assume that they would follow their profession, fitting into the grooves that had been worn by tradition and habit. There were continuities which could be counted on to support such a training. Today, however, the continuities are largely gone. History has changed color, taken a turn, and the work a minister must do in our time is not to be adequately described by what his predecessors did in the nineteenth century.

We may describe these new conditions any way we wish; but they are of the nature of a breathtaking apocalypse. The world, so to speak, has dislocated itself from both the classical and the biblical way of life. A new way of life, with its own presuppositions about the nature of reality, of man, of society, or morals, has become the ruling power of existence. It is rapidly unveiling its direction, its intent, its demands, and belatedly its dangers. Christendom as such is dead; a new technological civilization has taken its place. The Christian faith, in its traditional fashion, may continue to be practiced in small enclaves, as though the Victorian world still mothered it in a friendly environment. "We have run aground. Consequently our evangelism at present consists almost exclusively of superficial programs, of ecclesiastical coastal navigation, of spiritual suburban traffic." [1] But the break between the faith which believes in transcendent realities and the world which makes its own values is now blatantly plain. We would have seen it a long time ago had we not been so pleased to make the best of both worlds, but now the great divorce stares us in the face and will not be hidden.

Let it be said with honesty: theological education, despite

[1] J. C. Hoekendijk, "Die Theologie des 'vierten' Menschen," *Die Neue Furche,* 7:391–397 (1953).

its improved standards, has been the last of the professional fields either to feel the force of the modern revolution or to be willing to acknowledge it. Whereas radical changes have been made in all other professional schools, despite all our curriculum juggling, we still plod the old worn ruts. Medicine, education, business, languages, physics, art—all have been subject to a most perceptive scrutiny and careful reordering. In theology, we have had survey after survey, but no fundamental breakthrough to a new vision of how to prepare a minister to cope with the twentieth century, either in the tranquilized church or the terrified world. We are superb at the study of origins, excellent at unraveling history, erudite in matters of the past, sharp in analysis of ancient manuscripts, utterly fantastic in research, but how to get a man set up to function creatively in the service of humanity, precisely under the conditions presented by the present-day church and the current world, is another matter. One wonders, not cynically but in sad humility, can theological education be reformed? Dare we say that what has happened in every other field has no relevance for us? Are we really beyond the sea tides which have changed every social institution of our age? Should we continue to prepare men as if the shape of the church is going to remain unchanged? Is it enough for us to train men so that they will fit into the church as it is, quite stubbornly satisfied with itself, relatively undisturbed by the agony of the twentieth century?

There are three basic suggestions which I believe must enter into any radical reordering of our task. In the first place, theological disciplines must break out of their sacred isolation and meet modern man in the world where he is now living. Second, theological schools must recognize no terminal point in the training of ministers. Third, whatever integrity there is in the gospel, whatever continuity and perennial reality, we must prepare ourselves for deliberate flexible innovation in a rapidly changing context of culture and society.

Let us turn to the first condition. The basic fact of our dilemma, as Wilfred Cantwell Smith puts it, is that we have come to the end of religious isolationism—not only between Catholicism and Protestantism, but between the religion of the church and the religion of the world. The walls of partition were first undermined by the bold thrust of the Reformers, but slowly and inevitably the accumulating results of their courageous action have now blurred beyond recovery the fine line between God's action in the church and God's action in the world. They were the agents of dispersion by which men's eyes and hearts were opened to see and receive God's presence anywhere in the world. They broke the monopoly of the church; Protestantism has too often acted as if that had never been done. We now have reached the point where theology must do more than elaborate the nature of Christian faith within the church; it must interpret the religious significance of God's nonecclesiastical action in the world. Its proper function is to elicit the reality of God's grace in circumstances and events which seem to be quite secular.

We simply cannot continue to act as if the religious tradition is self-sustaining. The covert monasticism of Protestantism, slightly more veiled than the overt monasticism of the fifteenth-century Catholicism, must be breached, letting the world in and letting faith out. We need by some grace of courage to contrive new ways to get at the world, and new ways for the world to get at us, or else we shall be preparing a set of shrunken heads to run the specialized machinery of introverted churches. The tight walls which presumptively separate the various aspects of human life are showing signs of breaking down on all sides. As Karl Jaspers puts it:

The doctor, the teacher, the administrator, the judge, the clergyman, the architect, are each in his own way professionally concerned with man as a whole, and the conditions of life as a whole. Preparation for these professions is unthinking and inhuman if it fails to relate us to the whole and to develop our perceptiveness, to show the wide scope of knowledge, or to make us think philosophically.[2]

The implications of a renaissance of the arts to the basic images of religious thought and devotion, the sharp critique of pulpit language by analytical philosophy, the impact of dynamic psychology on rationalistic theology, the probing questions of existentialism for any realistic evangelism, the articulation of current forms of experience in the drama and novel for Christian anthropology, the questions posed by urbanization and mass media for ethics, the cry from business and industry for help in shifting from individualistic ethics to large corporate decisions, the influences of automation and the prevalence of technique on the human soul, the effect of mass media on the reflective habits and contemplative ideals, all these and more need to be brought into the active arena of our concern. Our theology programs need a thoroughgoing ventilation.

If, in this critical situation, the church is not ready to move into active dialogue with the world, and insists on perpetuating its own past, then the theological school must learn to speak directly with the world, respecting its hunger, its doubt, its agony, its questions, and its striving. All over the world, in business, in government, in art, in the sciences, in industry, there are men and women carrying the burden of this world's heaviest issues, its deepest embarrassments, its obvious shame,

[2] Karl Jaspers, *The Idea of the University*, Karl W. Deutsch, ed., Preface by Robert Ulich (Boston: Beacon Press, 1959), p. 47.

its awful fears, and its highest hopes. They are listening for the voice of honesty, of spiritual discernment, of persuasive compassion. As Jean Danielou, the Catholic scholar, points out:

In the broader view of our civilization, one of the features of the revival of religion is the religious feeling that is stirring today at the core of human concerns; we had been making religion too much something isolated; religion is stirring again at the very base of human activities; it is springing up again in scientific thought, inasmuch as the latter, in the course of its inventory of the cosmos, is feeling the need to go beyond itself; it is springing up again within the state, inasmuch as adoration, or the presence of God, appears today to be as substantially necessary to the common weal as are economic life and scientific progress.[3]

Let us speak directly to them out of every prophetic insight we may have, and be thankful that God has moved in their hearts, as we hope He has in ours.

In the second place, it is no longer possible to educate a man theologically to cope with this complex world in three years or in ten years. There simply is no longer a terminal date for theological training. The illiteracy of our present pulpit in America is a scandal, both to the churches which encourage it and to the schools which do little or nothing to change it. The ministry has lost, since the turn of the century, the dignity of intellectual leadership in American society.

One thing could be done and must be done. Men in the parish should be returned at regular intervals for sufficient time and serious study to sustain their morale and to increase their effectiveness. Industry does it; business does it; education does it. Why not the church? No profession needs it more, if it is to regain the vital nature of its professional competence.

[3] Jean Danielou, S.J., *The Scandal of Truth* (Baltimore: Helicon, 1962), pp. 127–128.

In the third place, training for the parish ministry must find a way to flex the muscles of a man's imagination and inventiveness in the practice of his craft. A long time ago, Alfred North Whitehead declared, "The fixed person for the fixed duties, who in older societies was such a godsend, in the future will be a public danger." The day for stupidly static forms placed indiscriminately by bureaucratic propaganda on all churches alike should be brought to an end. Planned innovation to fit the indigenous needs of a particular neighborhood or of a local situation must be foreseen as the normal procedure for the parish minister. Theological training that does less than prepare a man for such creative experimentation should be ashamed of itself.

The gist of this is that whether we train them for it or not, men are going into a world of insecurity—insecurity in the face of rapid change, insecurity in the wake of vast revolution, insecurity in the inevitable new forms of the church, insecurity in the shifting orders of belief and authority, insecurity in the loss of old landmarks, old labels, and old words, insecurity in the maze of new forms, new hopes, new visions.

To be sure, they need to be anchored more deeply than ever in the origins, but imaginatively, in order to see their modern manifestations; they need the past and need it desperately, not merely as research material, but as a way to understand the stubborn complexity of the present; they need traditions, but not as a masquerade in the midst of the violent anguish of mankind's new thrust for a better world; they need the objective sophistication of the scholar, but they need it to meet intelligently the complicated needs and bewildering power of our age.

Once in a while I lift my head from the cluttered workbench of my labors and catch a glimpse of a strange new world. I see the old wineskins, hard and cracked, but on a thousand hills the blue grapes shine in the warm sun and give promise of the new wine. I see the husk of old institutions, dry and lifeless, stacked up and crackling in an ecclesiastical babel higher and noisier than ever before, but all through the world, in the most unexpected places, among the most unlikely people, a light is shining. There is no sign on the door, no notice in the paper, no spire on the roof, no status sought, no privilege required. The light shines in the darkness, wavering with the wind and with its own mystery. How it came to be there, in such hearts and under such noncanonical conditions, only God knows. And all over the world, in cities and hills and forests, it would seem that some strange seed had broken from the dried husk of the church and had caught in the rough soil of the world, had found root in the godly depth of life, and grown like a flower in hearts surprised by it, hearts that scarcely knew their own hunger for it before it blossomed there and changed the air with its grace.

Everywhere the grace of God is breaking out of the world, from all its cracks and crannies, from what seemed a wilderness, a sheer desert, a waste place. The voices are shouting in drama, in politics, in the novel, in government, in the arts. It is as if the very stones had become disciples of a new life burgeoning mysteriously from the hidden power of the living God.

What security does a man want in a world that has awakened in such a way? How much will status satisfy him in a time when the light flashes from place to place in a thousand shelters across the hills, where the pilgrims of this restless day find a reason for their climbing and struggling? What craven hope is it that turns faith into a tranquilizing pill and the gospel into a nostalgic return to the safe piety of the nineteenth century? When Jesus was ordained, he went down into the market place; when the modern church recovers his gospel, it will do the same thing, and do it unashamedly, to sit with publicans and harlots to see what God's mercy has wrought in them. When he called men, he did not promise them security, but only that, like the son of man, they would find no place to lay their heads; yet their hearts would burn within them, and they would ask for no other peace than that which God gave them.

THE REFORM OF
THE MINISTRY

Everything else has been reformed, so it is not strange that we assume the ministry will be! The pressure to bring everything up to date, from automobile design to obstetrics, inevitably includes the ministry, despite the sanctity and conservatism which tend to cling to it. And no doubt the ministry needs reform. Indeed, there are moments when it seems like calling in a blacksmith with his horseshoeing tools to repair a jet engine or an electronic computer. The minister does not appear to be especially fitted, with his biblical quotations, fourth-century theology, and sixteenth-century church, to be able to deal very delicately or skillfully with the complicated twentieth century created by science and industry, and sophisticated by Marx and Nietzsche, Darwin and Freud.

But let us not make a very obvious mistake. In one sense, the ministry has already been reformed. In the last fifty years, it has undergone a severe and radical change. It may appear to the unobservant as much the same, but to a multitude of men caught in the forms of the inherited investiture, it is anything but the same! The minister tends to speak the same words, preach from the same Bible, conduct the same services, officiate in the same way at funerals and marriages, but under and through all these things the expectation of his congregation is quite different. He is evaluated not by these things at all. What they want of him has little or nothing to do with these things. They are part of the accidental furnishings of his job, like a spinning wheel in a split-level parsonage, or a barometer in an air-conditioned office! The truth is, the ministry has been transformed already. It has been secularized, at least

Address at 100th Anniversary of Grosse Pointe Memorial Church, Grosse Pointe, Michigan, November 7, 1965.

in the sense that what is expected of the minister is success. Almost anything can be forgiven, if he increases the size of the church, adds to its budget, expands its plant, and manages to be popular.

Most ministers come into the ministry by some experience or notion that they are to serve God. Undoubtedly that was the expectation generally believed even by congregations in times past. Today many ministers leave the ministry because they find no room for this peculiar misapprehension, and many remaining in it envy the honesty of secular callings, unattended by such irrelevant dreams.

The ministry has actually undergone a considerable change. It has been quantified, put under the prestige–success measure of our culture, submitted to social and administrative criteria. It is neither what it was nor what it should be. The declining ordination rate across the land—Protestant, Catholic, and Jewish—is an indication of widespread uncertainty about the feasibility of doing God's will in the ministry, under conditions dictated by ecclesiastical ideas of institutional success.

But what about the future? Obviously, there are drastic pressures which will continue to mount as society changes in this fast-changing epoch. One confronts such a question as the prediction of change, particularly in religious forms such as the church or the ministry, with considerable trepidation. History is notorious for its unexpected turns and twists; one can only expect the unexpected. Nevertheless, the future is hard upon us. The complex jumble of social revolutions now in progress forces its own inescapable questions upon us. The only help we may find is to discern some indication of what may determine the nature of the changes. If we can do this, we may be guided more dependably.

Whatever else may affect the ministry in the coming decades, the basic factor will be the new relationship between religion and the world. The most momentous fact of our time is the arrival of a self-consciously nonreligious culture. Previous ages saw many conflicts between religion and politics, trade and religion, religion and the arts; but under all the differences there ran certain common presuppositions about the nature of reality. Today the secular no longer accepts the premises of religion, namely, God, immortality, final judgment, salvation. The Christian faith no longer underlies science, industry, politics, or art. These have been secularized, separated from the Biblical tradition, independent of ecclesiastical pressure, and free to express themselves in their own right and by their own authority. Religion has a new relationship to the world, epitomized by the probing and problematic puzzles of theology stated by the ill-fated Bonhoeffer.

If the world decides that religion is a primitive hangover, or a medieval superstition; if it alienates itself from the heritage of its ancient origins; if it condescends to it as a weak and effeminate force in practical matters; if it twists it to suit its own purposes, then the minister may find himself isolated, restricted to the purely ecclesiastical, forced to operate monastically, if he is to be faithful in any sense of the word to his call as a servant of the Lord and of his gospel.

But if the world rediscovers the religious dimension of life itself; if it begins to see that religious reality is intrinsically involved in the world's concerns; if its search for meaning in the labors of our mortal life discloses the need for some kind of faith; if it tries to transcend the tragic, which inevitably pursues men, whatever their prestigious position in society or their salary level and success in business; if it finds out that the order and satisfaction of society are impossible without the aid of a social imagery which religion alone can supply, then the minister will not be the director of a monastic club of people who water down religion in order to keep it from any explo-

sive effect upon ordinary existence, but a public servant. He
will not be so much a chaplain of a private institution for
the "happy few" as a politician; he will serve the world as
loyally as he serves the church.

When Jesus was called of God to his ministry, he went into
the market place, not into the Holy of Holies. He found his
paradigms of God's acts, not in the rites of the temple, but in
the nonreligious activities of the shepherd, the merchant, and
the housekeeper. Of all the prophets, he was the most secu-
larly minded. He reconciled the ancient heritage of faith,
the God of Abram, Isaac, and Joseph, with the current world
of the tax collector, the Samaritan, and the harlot, with the
God hidden in the commonplace, the vulgar, and the routine.
It must be remembered—and never too often—that his ministry
was conducted where men worked, at the boats, in the markets,
near their shops, on the lake. On two occasions when he went
to the temple, the people attacked him in the first instance
and in the second he attacked them.

The basic change in the ministry, I believe, will be this
new orientation to the world. This will not mean that the
minister will diminish his loyalty to the church by increasing
his labors for the world. Indeed, he will be most faithful to
his charge to keep the church when he perseveringly serves
the world. He will fulfill his mission, not by increasing the size
of the ecclesiastical institution—that may decrease in order to
be what it ought to be. His call to be a public servant may,
for the first time in centuries, provide him with a reasonable
service for doing the will of God.

Let us ask more in detail what this reformation of the institutional pastor into a public servant means. In the first place,
it means the recovery of the "depth" of life in the world, of
discerning the kingdom of God within the ordinary occasions

of life, of recognizing the acts of God in the secular circumstances of common history, of discerning the sanctity of profane
callings and events. Whenever we want to define what is religious, we reach into the church for its artifacts—baptism,
eucharist, heaven and hell, savior, sacrament—as though these
were packaged and branded, bottled and dispensed, labeled
and guaranteed, while the rest of life provided no such meanings or revelations or satisfactions. The new public servant will
sharpen his sight and deepen his understanding in order to
read the daily page of human experience in such a way as
to uncover a deeper meaning than men, especially men in a
hurry, hunting for other things, suspected might be found.

Indeed, the public servant-minister will be called to articulate the dignity of the secular callings. Much of our present
world is disillusioned about the meaning of its work. Some
of it undoubtedly is worthless, from a human standpoint. But
the rehabilitation of social purposes, the substance of community, the ideal of human concern, all need to be elevated.
We need—and we need it desperately—to rediscover a new
depth in our secular activity. Put succinctly, we must discover
the acts of God in the non-ecclesiastical events of the world,
if our religion is to sustain its own truth or that of our civilization.

There is a feedback from this, of singular importance. It is
that any new depth discovered in our common life, in the
modern world, will open up new depths in the worship of God.
The liturgies are like old coins, so worn by handling that they
no longer reveal their intention or true value. The public servant will open up the meaning of the old, the primordial, the
myth, and the symbol, and show them to have been derived
from God's secular acts, from his ambiguous manifestations in
the flesh. When we touch the deepest things in the world,

then and only then shall we touch the deepest things in worship. We shall perceive that the public servant is and must be the servant of God.

In the second place, such a public servant must not only discover a new depth in the world, in order to sustain its meaning and dignity, but he must be able to pull the world together in a larger unity. It will not be enough to keep the religious vision of the first or twentieth century intact; he must boldly conceive of larger syntheses of thought and action for the twentieth.

For instance, he must move beyond the way in which Protestantism has tended to confuse the Christian ethic with middle-class mores. Not only have we made the Christian notion of goodness much smaller than it really is; we have deceived ourselves and put our ideals in place of Christ's. It may be hard, but we need to see that the Beatitudes simply cannot be cut out of the moral ideals of prosperity, success, optimism, and overproduction. We may have to do away with the Beatitudes—as we have in practice—in order to be honest, or we may have to repudiate some contemporary ideals in order to be Christian.

Moreover, there are many new demands upon us in regard to such a new world. Socially, we need to move beyond the limits of middle-class mores, beyond the limits of the white race, beyond the limits of inherited sectarianism, beyond the limits of Protestantism, if the Christian vision of the world is to be respected. The end of religious isolationism is here; nothing we can do now can avert it. All that is left is for us to deny it and hide our heads in the sand while it flows over and around us, or face it bravely, boldly, humbly, and creatively.

Along with the new dimensions of social concern, which the public servant-minister must espouse, are the new dimensions of truth. We have all kinds of truth, and all kinds of ways of expressing truth. We are sophisticated, in that science, art, religion, literature, philosophy have developed their own vocabularies and their own authorities. To be a whole man, to be all we can be as human beings, we need to embrace the various experiences of our diverse culture. All too often, science is accepted at the expense of religion. Science is accepted, but myth is not; Freud is accepted, along with Oedipus, but not Genesis! Not only is this confusing; it is depriving modern man of that full life in which he may recover a larger dimension and depth of meaning than the poverty-stricken fanaticisms or sectarianism which has heretofore permeated our culture.

In the third place, if the minister is to become a public servant, deepening the dimension of life in the secular order and creating a new synthesis of moral concern, both socially and intellectually, it is rather plain that he himself will be expected to change. To reform the ministry means inevitably to reform the minister! It may mean changing his ideals, his motivation, his sensibility, his direction, his hope, his satisfactions. He may have to rediscover biblical norms and standards, as over against the industrial ones which now rule the current scene. It may not be necessary for him to make his church as big as General Motors, or as efficient as IBM, or as powerful as the Federal Reserve, or as popular as the Beatles! Religion may not need to be as sure of itself as science, or as productive as industry, or as persuasive as advertising, or as universal as Coca Cola! The minister may have to rethink the place of religion in the world, and, with it, his own function; and, under that, what kind of person he ought to be.

For whatever may be said of the reform of the ministry, the revolutions of thought and action, of self and society, of church and the world, now in progress, all of them are changing the shape of human consciousness, the pattern of the person. The minister, if his ministry is to be reformed, will be reformed himself, and will look like a different man.

There are some indications of this in the ministry itself, and, equally significant, in the pages of contemporary novelists who are concerned with what it means in a world like this to be eminently human and to serve the highest needs of the race. One can see it in what I have called elsewhere "the reappearance of the saints." Novelists like Ignazio Silone and Morris L. West, dramatists like T. S. Eliot and Robert Bolt, have been interested in delineating figures who did not derive their actions from conformity to the prevailing styles of greatness. Whether the image we have contrived and clung to for a century or more is sufficient to sustain the larger orders of depth and unity to which I have called attention is seriously in doubt. We need a new kind of saint; a new kind of minister, if you will; in short, a new kind of man to admire and to emulate. Unless that be accomplished, the notion of religion will remain merely a notion, perhaps a very popular one, but scarcely more than a tranquilizer to quiet the nerves haunted by inflated unrealities.

In that kind of world, the minister cannot shelter himself in the church, or validate his role by its success. Perhaps the new man should be called a seer. After all, the modern world is giving evidence of extraordinary vitality in a thousand fields. It is anything but desolate. Violent perhaps, mad at times, inexplicably stupid, but everywhere, north, east, south, and west, on every continent, a wild conflagration of vigorous ideas, experimental activity, hopeful aspiration burns into human hearts at every level of society. The world is being reborn. And what is desperately needed is the kind of minister who makes an effort to sort it out, to shift the chaff from the wheat, to separate its substance from the shadows, to put his finger down where its truth can be affirmed, to point out the new forms of beauty which startle us, and to unveil the acts of compassion which invest the concerns of men in ways unseen before. He must become a public servant, ministering to the world which God "so loved that He gave His only begotten Son" for it. In its compromises, he will find a new Holy of Holies; in its routine, he will stumble upon many an epiphany; in its rude conditions, he will be called upon to recognize the word made flesh, the mercy of God in plain and unexpected places. The minister, like Christ, is sent into the world to identify the events through which God's love can be seen and confirmed.

THE UNEASY
FRONTIER

To read this age aright and not to be deceived either by its power and sophistication or by its violence and vulgarity is a task to stagger our intelligence and bewilder our comprehension. It is a fabulously rich world, rich in a thousand ways and in all directions. It is rich in its heritage, rich in its vitality, rich in its skills, rich in its massive wealth, rich in its ingenuity, rich in its diversity, rich in its freedom. And the very fact that it is so amazingly rich makes it a very confusing world. In that confusion religion shares.

History in our time seems to be tumbling over itself. With an increasing frenzy, the workshop of the world seems to be engaged in more jobs than it can handle. Plans are scrapped and models broken up before the product is half done. Revolutions occur so fast that one can scarcely tell which is revolt and which is counterrevolt. The status quo is gone; the settlement never occurs. Everything is in flux; change itself is the new order; the expected routine is the ceaseless shifting of routine. Nothing rests.

What this does to institutions, all institutions from the family and the state to religion, is so profound and so complicated that it is difficult to assess or to define with accuracy. Continuities are desolated, traditions are fractured, communications are obscured, origins are lost, words slip, slide, and change their meanings; symbols and waymarks lose their shape; the common ritual binding society together disappears, the images of memory or of hope are twisted and junked. The human

Given at a meeting of the American Association of Theological Schools, June 9, 1966, and published in *Horizons of Theological Education,* John Coburn, Walter Wagoner, and Jesse Ziegler, eds. (American Association of Theological Schools, 1966).

landscape becomes bizarre, both desolate and crazy, emptied and crowded, void and leaping with activity. Things are turned upside down; what looks like faith is merely the hard wineskin now devoutly adored for its sure shape and definability, while unfaith struggles boldly with the absence of order in the passionate assurance of finding a new center. Compassion moves under new names and with banners of political or scientific slogans, while the professional agents scratch each other's backs for a measure of indulgent comfort. The maps, both geographical and spiritual, no longer tell the truth about the city of man since it was bombed, demolished, and rebuilt by the frenzy of the new age.

Religion in such a rich and at the same time surrealist world of immense new freedoms, as well as striking self-induced neuroticisms, can scarcely remain untouched. It is possible, as some will try, to encapsulate it, to make a relic of the holy faith, as some have kept bones or splinters or blood of the crucifixion. But for the most part it will change, simply because it is an aspect of our human condition, and more profoundly, I believe, because God moves in each succeeding age to act with unprecedented novelty and meaning. The living God is never served by a static faith; a single act in the long history of the world does not adequately testify to His infinite power and wisdom.

To find our way in this age, where we have been born, to do it discerningly, separating the wheat from the chaff, to discover the possible foundations in it which will sustain faith, to elicit from its mysteries and contradictions some solid sense of meaning, and to open up in the long dimensions of history some direction and destiny for our place in it as human beings is, I take it, part of our religious responsibility. I see no indication that God introduced religion as a pill to cure the world long after its creation. It is intrinsic to the nature of life and not an import. The spirit of man is neither an enemy of his body, nor is his body an enemy of his spirit, however much they struggle in tension with each other to sustain his creativity. Neither is religion the opposite of the world, unless the latter term is used figuratively to describe something less than creation; nor is the world so hostile to religion that religion can afford to withdraw from its demands and agonies. The proper task of the church, the seminary, and the ministry is to find the path in the world that leads to man's fulfillment as a child of God, however obscure, tangled, and tortured the way may be. The world is not so neatly exorcised by turning our back on it, no matter how pure our motives may be or however ascetic our discipline is. We carry the world in us, and our faith cannot be separated from it.

The point of our probing, then, rests on what Hegel called defensively "the terrible principle of culture." It is the general ground of our existence with all its manifold meanings, inheritances, conditions, and directions. It cannot be simplified, especially in the later stages of civilization, when accumulations of historic styles from many different epochs diversify the nature of our experience. It is a moving, dynamic, often contradictory, highly problematic environment where much is taken for granted, many factors assume the rigidity of law, and others by their strangeness excite our fears and fill us with dread. In this matrix, the culture of the world, of this human life, the church and the seminary must work out their understanding of their mutual relationship as they seek to uncover the ways of God to men living now in this kind of world.

Something of the relationship between the church and the seminary may be paralleled by the situation in medicine or in law. In medicine, the school acts as a research and teaching organ, while exerting a continuous pressure on the level of professional care offered by the hospital. In law, the school likewise serves as an instrument of research and teaching, while effecting an intense pressure on the courts and the exercise of justice. In religion, the situation can scarcely be generalized. For the most part, the seminary seems to exert little or no direct pressure on the churches at all. The very wide influence of Reinhold Niebuhr on industrial and business leaders, and the similar influence of Paul Tillich on intellectuals in many fields, affected the churches not at all. Denominational seminaries provided the kind of ministers the churches wanted, or if they moved much beyond that, the democratic processes soon conditioned their graduates to conform if they expected either to stay or to advance. Generally, it is hard to distinguish any effect the seminaries have had on the life of the churches. Indeed, if there has been any pressure at all, it has been in the opposite direction: churches keeping the seminaries as close to their own line as possible!

The point of issue is not long revealing itself. It is simply that the kind of ministers the churches want is not the kind the seminaries want to give them. This is not the result of any overt hostility, but simply because the seminary is predominantly an educational institution and the church a social one; in the former, the scholar is the ideal; in the latter, a pastoral leader. The search for a bridge of accommodation is not easy to find.

The responsibility of both seminary and church is the redemption of "the times," or to deal creatively with the culture in which it finds itself. To assume that it can justify its place in the economy of history by paying attention to itself as a discrete element in the nature of things and to justify this as fidelity to God, I believe is a dangerous subversion of faith as well as of truth. The effort is often made, and not always without the appearance of some historic validity, that there are times when religion is preserved only by paying attention to itself. At such times it is assumed that one goes back and forth from religion to politics, or to art, or to the sciences, much as one goes from house to laboratory or market place.

And this in the smaller cycles or patterns of dialectic is true and meaningful. But the basic ground of all these interactions is in culture, and it is here that the reality of meaning must be elicited and a style of life established. If the separations grow too wide, or the contradictions too violent, life itself becomes schizophrenic, unbearable, and men retreat to smaller areas, where they can control the consistency of life.

Moreover, if Christianity is really what it purports to be, namely, an historical religion, or even as some put it, *the* historical religion, then it can scarcely risk the solecistic reduction of the faith to a single period on which everything hangs. As Trilling clearly expressed it: "The refinement of our historical sense means that we must keep it properly complicated." The structures of time and history are complicated; no more so than when we seek to derive faith from its mysterious origins in the imaginative structures we inherit or the complex of empirical happenings which occur freshly in the living day.

However the situation is viewed, the essential problem in church and in seminary is culture, that ambience of all things visible and invisible, the general habit of life and thought in which we live and by which we are conditioned. What are the marks of its character, the style and shape of its quality, the stance and direction of its major concerns? Are these characteristics favorable or unfavorable to the nurture of faith, and in which ways do they exert pressure, both on the individual and on the institutions of religion?

Modern culture is characterized by two component elements operating with profound and cumulative effect upon each other, namely, the scientific and the industrial. They constitute the theory and practice of modern life. Together they create a technical culture, preponderantly committed to the way of techniques as a method of solving the problems of every conceivable field, even the arts, prayer, and love. Out of this technical culture a specific type of society has evolved, which we call the city. In a cultural sense, the city marks the character of the whole society, for though there may be agricultural and rural areas not congested as the former, yet their life is also "urbanized" by the effects of mechanization, transportation, and communication. All the institutions of society, from the basic family to the large, generalized form of government are profoundly altered by these forces, and indicate by their changes subservience to them. The sociological conservatism of church and seminary stands in marked contrast to other institutions. A heavy inertia lies upon both seminary and church. While other professions have radically altered their training of candidates over the last fifty years, the seminary has not. And the church still remains much as it was when it congealed in the first phases of the Reformation, three centuries ago. A great deal of "surveying" and much tinkering with small repairs have gone on for a long time in the seminaries, but no major change to bring them into realistic contact with the new age has occurred. In general, the institutions of religion have become as monastically separated from the prime questions of our day as the monasteries of the medieval world were walled off from the rising vitality of the sixteenth and seventeenth centuries. The gathering forces of disillusionment and the growing urgency of a fresh renewal of faith presuppose a radical reformation as bold as Luther's and as comprehensive as Augustine's.

Let us look more closely at the character of modern culture and its effect upon religion. The climate of man's mind and heart, created by the force of science and industry and institutionalized in the social conditions of life in the city, has assumed an ideological character. It is the natural reflection of that organization principle by which his world is held together and by which it operates. It produces timetables and bureaucracies, moon shots and assembly lines, military logistics and computers. It is basically a replacement of direct feeling by abstractions, of immediate reactions by generalized concepts, of contents by forms. It is a kind of intellectual technique, by which the concrete and the empirical tend to be put into the distance and the conceptual formulates their place and function, but always at a discreet distance from which they can be judged, controlled, and to that degree deprived of their intrinsic power of impact.

The literature of our culture reflects this general character. On the one hand it is filled with men fascinated by the pursuit of ideas, once removed from reality, which they collect with a kind of intellectual lust. Perhaps Pecuchet and Bouvard, that pair of Flaubert's cockroaches, are the prime example. But our novels are filled with such kind—giving rise to the category so prevalent now, of "alienation." These are the ideologically alienated, those who have reached the higher stories of verbation and cannot find the way back to earth. Joyce and Nietzsche, Eliot and Orwell, Dickens and Henry James, all delineated in various ways this endemic trait of technical culture. And, on the other hand, we have plenty of examples of those who, having felt the estrangement of this attic-mentality, sought violently to re-establish their connection with the vital immediacies of existence. Indeed this is especially true of our American scene, where Whitman and Hemingway, William James and John Dewey, and a host of lesser lights, by giving us the ruder side of life thought they were restoring us to reality. All in all, we have discovered that ideological excesses may land us in as much pain and confusion as sheer lust of the flesh.

Indeed, the effect of this ideological condition of modern culture is quite obvious. If it pushes things and events into a convenient distance where they can be handled in a safe and sterile fashion, by the very act it separates the self from its normal matrix. The safety gained may be small advantage in the light of ungrounding the self and thus subjecting it to the agonizing and futile effort to be self-supporting. Self-identity is not to be attained in a vacuum, nor are ideas capable of sustaining life. Nothing is more widely attested to in the literature of the last three hundred years, or in the contemporary world of psychic crises, than the severe ordeal which the self has undergone in our time. Shakespeare and Goethe prophetically indicated the struggle in *Hamlet* and *Faust,* but since then the line of pilgrims has thickened until all of us today feel the inexorable pressure which Freud clinically described of this basic warfare between the self and society.

The impact of this on religion is not to be overestimated. If there is one place in man's many-leveled life where immediacy is of the essence of truth, it is religion. All of it strives for a complete rejection of all subterfuges, circumlocutions, façades, and masks. What is required is nothing less than the open heart, the true self, the undisguised soul—repentance, purity, trust, all in genuine terms and without hidden tricks. The spirit is itself conceived as truth, the essence of the man, revealed before the awfulness of God's perfect knowledge. In short, religion loses its very foundation, its nurturing ground when man or society, church or seminary, ascends into safe abstractions of the ideological realm. One can talk about religion then, without restraint, without fear, without embarrassment. This indeed was Kierkegaard's lament, that we had reduced faith to verbiage and that it had literally run wild.

If one turns this, then, to the seminary, one is forced to ask a very serious question. What is the distinction between the ideological subversion of faith and the intellectual fulfillment of it? A seminary is an educational institution, by nature formulated to discuss and transmit ideas, both to enlarge the natural horizon of young minds and to fit them for a more comprehensive practice of directing both their own and others' religious activities. Generally speaking, instruction in religion has become almost entirely historicized, that is, it has been granulated in terms of its historical development, major figures, and systems of ideas. Just as art, in most universities, becomes not the practice of it but only its history, so in most seminaries the method at hand is to reduce faith to the easiest form of its transmission, namely, the idea, especially the idea which has a history, can be documented, and bears its appendage of footnotes!

How far this can be called ideological and how far intellectual is hard to say. The pressures in theological education on both sides of the line are powerful and may in time break into public controversy, just as they did in the modernization of medical education. What is plain, however, at the present juncture, is that the kind of education being offered scarcely prepares a man for the kind of religious agony existing in the soul of modern man. It is not so much that the first century is treated with such scholarly thoroughness, or that the sixteenth century is scrutinized with such meticulous care. That has its proper integrity and ought not to be relaxed or lessened one whit. But the question that will not down is how the man so capably trained in the first or sixteenth centuries will be able to discern the twentieth. What are the relationships and the discontinuities between those documented times and our own as yet undocumented ones? Are there not dimensions and categories other than the historical that need to be included in the examination of religion? Can faith be adequately considered without a much more rigorous and extended curriculum of practice than now prevalent? Is it not true that some ideas in religion, as in art or medicine, simply cannot be "understood" unless the consciousness is stretched by personal involvement?

I am not suggesting that we retreat from this ideological condition of affairs, as if the intellectual part of faith were to be avoided. What I am suggesting is that we must not allow the ideological to presume itself both sufficient and adequate to represent Christianity. Indeed Christianity is really something else: it is the discipline of the whole life of man by which the innermost self is reached and the meaning of the world is elicited by a reconciling and fulfilling experience. The intellectual has its place in this discipline, and a most important and significant place, but in no sense is it the sovereign ruler whose law is absolute. There is something both elusive and authentic, both subtle and as firm as the mountains, in the gospel which makes the wisdom of the Greeks to appear as foolishness.

One thing that is rapidly forcing this fact upon our attention is the state of mind in which many men begin their seminary training. A generation ago, they came with their faith set, their vocational intention firm, their image of the ministry clear, and their confidence in the church unshaken. None of these things is any longer true. They are neither sure of themselves nor of their call, nor of their future, nor of the world. They share in the uneasiness, the alienation, the dread, the insecurity of their time. Putting the finest education in the world about the manuscripts of the gospel, or about the theological acuity of Calvin, on top of that foundation does not make a minister, though it might make a scholar. They represent the modern age more than the heritage from which it has largely disengaged itself. They are its ideological tramps, refugees, pilgrims. The very assumptions of our seminaries must be reoriented, not merely to confront the culture of our world but to deal honestly and creatively with the men we are training as directors of human faith, seers of God's mercy.

As for the church, the impact of the ideological is patently different. Here a vast ignorance prevails, not only about the development of the faith in its intellectual and historical terms, but more fundamentally about the very origins and sources of the Christian faith. There is little or no real tradition as such left. The havoc wrought by the excesses of pietism, reinforced

as it was by a general anti-intellectualism, devastated the
American church and left it an empty vacuum largely filled
with a spurious vagueness about Christian doctrines and un-
disciplined activism of the industrialized middle-class virtues.
The mores of the business world took over and provided the
motivations and satisfactions of the church in its hunger for
success and prestige. The result of these varied factors is a
medley of uninformed Biblicism as rigid as it is vague, a very
proper pose of respectability which has nothing to do with
Christian righteousness, and a powerful push for aggrandize-
ment. If there is anything ideological, it is simply that the
tradition embedded in the public language of the church has
little or nothing to do with its activities. Likewise, the realities
which stand behind the scriptural origins of the church have
lost their connections with the ordinary events of the daily
routine in people's lives. They have become a little like a coat
of armor which a man may greatly admire but which he
finds very few appropriate occasions to wear. Or, as Hendrik
Kraemer once put the matter: "The great Biblical key ideas
of sovereign divine creation, of covenant, election, sin, mercy,
judgment, conversion, rebirth, reconciliation, justification, sanc-
tification, Kingdom of God, are utterly alien, and consequently
irrelevant, to people whose minds are molded and dominated
by the conquest of the kingdom of man. They are undecipher-
able hieroglyphs, with which, strangely enough, Church people
still seem to play." [1]

I should like to raise a second question, not altogether unlike the first, regarding the "terrible principle of culture," as
it affects the nurture of those conditions in which religion
may be hospitably accommodated or rudely resisted. What
does modern technical culture, with its dynamics of science,
industry, and urban society, do to man's sensibilities? Does it

[1] Hendrik Kraemer, *The Communication of the Christian Faith* (Phila-
delphia: Westminster Press, 1956), p. 94.

condition him negatively or positively in respect to faith and the practices of faith?

In every age, embarrassed by the incongruities between its heritage and the common way of life (and none more than our own), religion has a hard time of it. Because it is intrinsically conservative, that is, deeply aware that the past has its proper validity and meaning for the present, and therefore is not to be cast off as obsolescent, there is a temptation to revert to it as if it had the whole truth and could provide firm ground against the winds and tumult of the present age. Or, on the other hand, it seems so antiquated, so befogged with primitive superstition and credulity, that there seems no reason to keep it amid the much more intelligent world which has come into being.

Underneath these natural extremes, however, there is another and more serious conflict. Whether faith leans more to the past or to the present, the new climate of life and thought determines the character of the questions which faith must confront. In our culture' for instance, the way in which all our energy, for over three hundred years, has been poured into paying strict and undiluted attention to the contingent structures of the natural world is something so extraordinary, so massive, that it is hard to comprehend it in its total magnitude. The whole tidal force of our imagination, our vision, our intellectual curiosity, has accumulated until we are passionately preoccupied with little else. In industry, a similar obsession has taken place; with mounting power and effectiveness we have increased our production of things until the frenzy of making them outdistances the real needs of men and we are forced to introduce "built-in obsolescence" in order to satisfy the egregious demand of the system. Both in science and in industry man's desires, material and intellectual, have reduced his vision of life to a slit-eyed view of the contingent, and have forced that to an even shorter span than nature would allow.

Given such conditions, it does not seem strange at all that God is no longer a viable reality. Neither in science nor in industry does the question of God rise from the nature of the activity. He simply does not fall within the purview of either one or the other, and for the most part for three centuries we have not been interested in anything else. We may debate the "death of God" theologically, or try to disengage and disentangle the concept by means of logical analyses, but the question is not fundamentally philosophical at all. It is simply and profoundly that we are conditioned and trained by three centuries of the most energetic and persevering discipline to look in one direction for one thing, and God is not in that field of vision. We have progressively and patiently, not knowing what we were doing, alienated ourselves from the kind of experience in which God might have been revealed.

And while science and industry in their total exercise give the appearance of monopolizing the whole area of human concern, nevertheless in actuality they are essentially *narrow* fields. The potential of experience is much wider. And there are signs that we may be beginning to feel the unwise constriction of life to its technical limitations. There is a growing dissatisfaction with our culture, despite its boisterous prosperity, which can be seen at every level of society and in varying degrees from harmless hobbies and the resurgence of crafts and the arts all the way to beatniks, hippies, Zen, violence, and suicide. There is more depth and more height to this world than we have explored in our recent search for facts and facture. The problem for the church and seminary is to reactivate dimensions of the human heart now somewhat atrophied. It will scarcely be done either at the level of ideological training or of building campaigns. It requires a new gambit, more fraught with mystery and the tangled fire that lies at the center of our souls.

It is here that one moves into the second area, where the

technical culture raises questions for the Christian. I take it that the most significant act in Christian faith is worship. This is the celebration of God's living presence in the world. It is a reminder of the epiphanies through which He has revealed Himself, a ritual by which the spirit of man is deepened and heightened to its full potential as child of God and brother of all men, a structure of symbols in which the tensions and contradictions of this life are embraced, and if not resolved, at least articulated, an affirmation of faith in which man puts himself at the disposal of that mercy and power which he believes can bring all things to their fulfillment; in short, it is an act by which the meaning of life shines through all its obscurity and tragic pain to glorify the Maker of it.

Now this is certainly not in the same key as science and industry. Two things constitute the difficulty of reconciliation; one, the reflective attitude of worship, and two, the nature of the symbols involved. In the first case, as much as our technical culture is highly sophisticated, it is basically nonreflective. Its very ideological character makes quantitative acquisition of facts possible without any serious concern for what anciently passed for wisdom. The very speed which now infects every portion of our existence, from transportation and communication to education and the use of leisure, has become compulsive and we are habituated to the "cinematic," restless vision which leaps from moment to moment, scene to scene, person to person, with no time or effort to penetrate anything deeper than the most superficial contact. Indeed, our lives are so frenetic that the only way we seem to pay any attention to the meaning of what we experienced is to lie on the couch of the psychiatrist and allow a highly paid professional guide us backward through half-lived events to recover their inner content and vital significance. A way of life (born of science and industry), however sophisticated and prosperous, which denies us the true savor and knowledge of our own life, is stupid at best and lunatic at its worst. And if we do not know how to reflect upon our existence or to elicit from it the hidden meaning of it, there is not much likelihood that worship will have more than an air of unreality about it, a kind of fastidious boredom.

The second place in worship where the waters meet in a violent eddy because they are not headed in the same direction is in the nature of symbols. To begin with, there are no symbols derived from the technical culture sufficiently comprehensive to articulate the mysteries which are affirmed in worship. The symbols of science and industry, or of the technology they have produced, *are* technical and not humanistic. The mysteries involved in the act of worship are not technical; they concern the paradoxes of God and the world, sin and forgiveness, freedom and necessity, law and grace, life and death, birth and rebirth, creation and redemption, body and soul, secular and sacred. These realities, which religion calls mysteries, will not fit into the simplified logic, or the mechanical models, or the advertising stereotypes of our technical imagination. The primordial myths, the originative revelations, the accumulative symbols of faith are of such magnitude as to make them virtually unmanageable to the technically trained mind. Worship has been scrapped, or endured, in modern culture, not because of its untruth, but because its vision is outside the usual purview of the modern mind.

On the other hand, the forms of worship are in grave need of revision. Whitehead's warning that every society needs to maintain its symbolic structure and at the same time revise it is timely. The church has failed since the Reformation to work at the difficult job of revising the imagery by which the new dimensions of man's thought and consciousness might be included.

Along with the problem of God, and the demands of worship, there is a third area where religion and the contemporary culture meet in ethics. There is little doubt about the prevalence of middle-class mores with their emphasis in appearance rather than being, and the preponderance of the aggressive virtues over the receptive ones. Most of the ideals now regnant in the church and seminary, apart from the general notion of love and service, stem from the Renaissance and the Industrial Revolution. It would be easy to compile a new set of ideals and match them one for one against the Beatitudes, which have not only been replaced but rendered quite unintelligible by the technical culture of our day. Blessed are the poor makes no sense to people whose life is spent in pursuit of more and more prosperity. Blessed are the meek has lost all meaning in a situation where ambition and a strenuous effort are made to dominate larger and larger fields of operation. One could go on, for in every instance the classic understanding of the Christian in the Sermon on the Mount is contraverted by our present understanding of what it means to be fully a man.

The major task of both church and seminary is the recovery of an authentic way of life, free from the compulsiveness of technical civilization, free from the boredom of superficial sophistication, and free from the spurious peace of the consciously saved.

In all three areas, neither seminary nor church is doing much to confront the religious issues which stem from living in this kind of world. How to express the reality of God with excitement for an age of sophisticated boredom, or how to fashion worship to recover the lost skill of reflection, or how to distinguish between the spurious virtues of getting ahead in the world and a true ethic of human integrity, would appear to be at least the beginning of a new Reformation.

It is not as if the church or the seminary did not have the resources for such a Reformation in its heritage. The trouble is, they remain buried in the heritage and require a new measure of boldness and a higher degree of imagination to dig them out and set them loose for their constructive work in the world than seems to be available at the moment.

Certainly a new level of professional competence will be required of the ministry if it is to serve the world and the church at the levels I have suggested. Any attempt to delegate his function to the laity in the mistaken notion that to be professional in religion means to be less than sincere, is subversive. The complexity and subtlety of the religious issues in contemporary culture are of such magnitude that only a much higher and more rigorous discipline is necessary to train men with the theory and skill sufficient to allow them to stand beside the finest scientists and the best physicians of the day. Anything less leads to a sloppy conformity to the haphazard moods and fads of amateurs whose perspectives are brief, personal, and local. No calling of our day is in greater need to be trained more rigorously in professional competence than the ministry.

There is a phrase from Yeats in which he yearns "to bring back the old disturbed, exalted life, the old splendor." Nostalgic as it may seem, the phrase is not without cogency in the field of religion. The age is stupendous, exciting beyond description, and desperately hungry for something that will reach down into the solid substance of reality, something that will touch us wide awake, drive the shadows from our eyes and the fears from our hearts, and bless us unmistakably at the sure center of our hearts. We may not welcome it, either in the sacrosanct air of the church or in the traditional custom of the seminary, but there is nothing we want more at bottom than to see the gospel come clean of all its fantastic wraparounds, and to be able to declare it in such a way as to make welcome news to men hungry for a larger truth than they have found in the laboratory or the market place.

TESTING MEN FOR
A NEW AGE

*A*new age demands new men. Whenever civilization achieves new dimensions of power, or society moves into greater complexity, then new kinds of persons are required. Everybody is tested in a thousand ways, and those who are able to stand the impact and bear the burden are pushed into the front line of leadership to guide and control the destinies of such an age. No one is exempt from the testing, though some may fear it and find ways to hide from it. The new world, now aborning, with its space craft and computers, artificial organs and floating cities, will insist on our adjustment to new levels of human endurance.

We are all being tested. When astronauts go into training for the moon shot, they consent to test the limits of stress and strain in the unprecedented pressures of rocket speeds and space travel. They are accelerated, spun centrifugally, endure weightlessness, and bear the brunt of deceleration far beyond the normal demands of routine existence. When we prepare ourselves for the 1970's and 1980's, we must be ready to reckon with the limits of mental stability, of personal integrity, which the violent thrust of social changes will threaten in the revolution of traditional ways of life. What will happen to the ordinary citizen may not be as dramatically demonstrable or as visible as what happens to the spacemen who land on the moon but the shock of such radical changes in our way of life may culminate in greater terror and more fundamental need of courage.

When Jesus confronted the rich young ruler, he was facing a man whose place in society was firm and unquestioned.

Given at a meeting of the Chicago Sunday Evening Club, March 7, 1965.

Indeed, the young man appears somewhat stuffy, to say the least. He had kept the law from his youth up. He had conformed to society, obeyed his parents, achieved a respectable reputation. There was evidently nothing to confess, no smudge on the record to be ashamed of. In fact, the Lord had rewarded him with great wealth. The word of Jesus, which rudely shattered the perfect picture, was simply that he lacked one thing: he was indecently adjusted to the past; he felt no insecurity for the present. If he were to enter into the full understanding of what it was to be a human being, responsive to the forces of history and the possibilities of a new age, he needed to get rid of whatever it was that kept him from being tested for a larger role, a more difficult destiny than the status quo.

The question of testing men for a new age is plainly not one I have invented. You can find it articulated in practically every business magazine in the country. Every year the mainspring of industry gets tightened a little more, the tension is increased, a 5 per cent increase over last year is expected, higher dividends are necessary, a bigger market must be found. Have we the nerves, the steady poise, the clear-eyed judgment to stand up under the pressure of new pressures, of demands made by the machines that control our business, of changes and complications that keep us in a constant nightmare of dread and anxiety?

Let us not underestimate the situation. The vast power we already have is being rapidly escalated. The speed at which we travel and by which our work is being done is being accelerated. The changes which keep us nervous and unsettled are nothing compared to the incessant movement easily discernible in the kaleidoscopic mobility of moods and fashions and the changing nature of jobs and professions which the future holds. The not yet realizable fact of doubling the population of the world in the next fifty years, the rise to independent power of the black and yellow races, who far exceed the white race in numbers, the increasing fanaticism of politics, with its psychopathic and paranoid potential, the precarious balance in which we hold the awesome power of the nuclear bomb in a world of tempestuous tempers and flaring hatreds—all this must be carried, and carried with patience, discrimination, and social forbearance. The burden will be incalculable, the strain will be unrelenting, the risk will be enormous.

Let us look briefly at four areas where we are being tested for the new age. The first question is: Can we match the technological unity of the world with enough moral imagination to keep it from exploding in war or in racial strife? We have united it, by the remarkable achievement of radio, airplane, the distribution of goods, and the dispersion of engineering know-how. It is one world, held forcibly together despite its prejudices, its hate, its injustices, and its fears—by an invisible network of airwaves and a visible network of transportation—but the fabric is as fragile as our moods and as explosive as our fears. Our hearts have not been as large as our greed; our good will has not stretched as far as our broadcasts. Until we can put under the technological fabric a foundation of emotional stability and moral justice sufficient to give all people an equal chance for dignity and a decent life, that technical unity will only be a source of dread and possible disaster. Until we can move into a moral covenant of respect for all mankind, we are a virulent danger to the new world. New men, with hearts hospitable to the whole world, will be able to sustain the superstructure of technical unity we have already built by the hands of science and industry.

The second question which will be asked in testing us for a new age is simply: Can we match the accelerated changes which now pervade our whole culture with sufficient integrity to establish a sane society? How much change can we stand before both the order of society and the inner balance of the individual are destroyed? If integrity was once associated with an established habit, repeated dependably over and over again, it will have to be reformed to maintain its dependability by flexibly changing with conditions and yet always confirming that which is morally right in the situation. Keeping the law, as with the rich young ruler, if it is merely a stereotype of past tradition, may be of all things the most immoral, if it fails to meet the new actualities of life. Our most difficult job today, morally speaking, is to translate the probity of our forebears into the kind of moral action demanded by conditions they never foresaw. Changes are occurring so fast and so furiously that it will take the most dogged perseverance and the most imaginative flexibility to keep our ship pointed true north. Any old direction will obviously bring disaster, but the blindness that thinks we need not change the sails or head her into a changing blow will be equally disastrous.

For instance, the individualistic ethic of the nineteenth century is no longer adequate for the implications of vast corporate decisions in the complex business milieu of today; the encouragement of prolific families a hundred years ago in a rural and agricultural epoch may have made sense but with the population explosion it no longer does, and some kind of control is inevitable; the work ethic, which has conditioned our sense of usefulness, is no longer adequate in a world of enlarging margins of leisure; political isolationism could be argued in the nineteenth century, but in a world of nuclear bombs and universal markets in business it is not only long gone by, but irrecoverable. Changes are incessant and the way of the new world. Whether we can keep our character under such conditions remains to be seen.

The third question in preparing for this new age is whether

we can match its superficial efficiency with an equally profound humanity. We are tempted by the excitement of speed to cover a great deal of territory without penetrating it very deeply. We hurry overmuch, but we do not reflect on anything very long. We rush headlong from one event to another, without staying with anything long enough to find out its meaning or what truth or beauty might be in it. We take our cue from the movies and are everlastingly flitting from one scene to another, distracted, as T. S. Eliot says, from distraction by distraction, until our lives fall apart in pieces. Technologically, this is a magnificent world, dazzlingly efficient, incredible in its speed, and as disconnected and chaotic, humanly speaking, as a gibbering lunatic. If you do not believe it, go to a cocktail party!

Can we match this on-the-surface speed with in-the-depth reflection? Can we collect our wits, sharpen the focus, pay attention to something or someone long enough to discern the mystery and to share in the quiet and hidden glory? Can we fall back from our supersonic flight from ourselves to rest in the human tempo of our more modest souls and learn somehow to be fully at home to one another when we meet and talk and love?

Finally, the fourth question is whether we can maintain our religious faith while living in a technological culture. Religion as we know it is being harshly tested by the technological culture of our day; perhaps we should not be averse to testing the technological culture by our religion!

In the first place, the primary mysteries of human life are not articulated or illuminated by the technological apparatus of science or industry. Birth and death, love and hate, sin and sanctity, joy and tragedy—these remain as they were in the days of Troy or the fall of Rome. No metaphor from the machine, no technique of manipulation, no analysis by X-ray or measuring of galactic space, brings us one whit closer to the human heart. It may shred man's flesh from his bone, grind his skull to powder, beat his blood to a froth, measure chromosomes and genes, but the mystery of self-identity, the ancient splendor of the soul, evades it all. The meaning of human life is not given by the machine, or any combination of machines, or any refinement of the machine.

In the second place, neither society nor the individual can maintain sanity, or coherence, or order, except by reference to the symbols of faith which have nothing to do with techniques of control or the technology of industry, but only with the ineradicable and often contradictory meanings of our human existence in life and death, in joy and sorrow, in good and evil. This is where the human speaks of realities of which the machine knows nothing and can know nothing. This is where faith may save the world made by machines, but machines will never save the world of men.

In the third place, there is laid upon us the desperate and critical necessity to conserve the full measure of the human self in the face of a burgeoning reverence for mechanical intelligence, a pseudo-intelligence, which to many seems to promise some easy salvation. If novels and plays and psychiatry have any testimony in common, it is the evidence that the self is having a tough time in our century to maintain its identity. For a century the grinding attrition excited by a powerful combination of impersonal forces has left all of us struggling to keep the semblance of our human sensibilities alive and responsive. Gabriel Marcel has categorized these forces as "the techniques of degradation," while contemporary literature has dramatized the human consequence as the non-hero, caught in a non-drama, without plot or meaning.

In conclusion, then, faith has a major job on its hands. It may choose to retreat and take cover in the comfortable shelters of creeds and convictions achieved by men in earlier ages.

That may keep the church intact, much as a museum is kept intact and guarded against human touch or rough usage, but it will not help the world or redeem it. A bolder conscience is required, a more profound obedience to God's will, namely to engage in the world, at the very edge of its dangerous and problematic progress, where change is forcing a new world on us, whether we like it or not. Unless we can identify the good in it, separate it from the evil, confirm the positive and suppress the destructive, unless we can recognize the signs of God's actual presence in this new world and greet the evidence of his work in it with discrimination and rejoicing, no amount of historical affirmation in the first century or the tenth will suffice. We are being tested, not to live under the Roman Caesars but in the midst of vast revolutions in space travel, in the social order, in the changes of life and work, in the loss of meaning and the attrition of the self, in the age of anxiety and of loneliness—is our faith strong enough not merely to endure it blindly, but to see God's will in it creatively?

Do not underestimate the magnitude of this struggle, nor the burden of its responsibilities. We shall be working at a huge task, with nothing less than the redemption of three centuries of history in which the aggressive powers of man have been unfolded and pushed to the limit. It will require a new birth of courage, a new level of faith, a new scope of vision. False fashions, spurious sophistication, scientific superstitions, ecclesiastical sentimentalities, social illusions, and popular credulity will have to be cast off. Fears and uncertainties, risk and nostalgic memories, pretentious hopes and all too human longings, will vie to tempt the tired spirit. A new world is coming to birth, fraught with great danger and great blessing, and in the travail the decisive factor will be whether man himself can be reborn—fit to match the new age with the strength of a larger and deeper soul.

Index